Be well, work smart, have f
fml --

FULL
life
BALANCE:

The 5 Keys to the Kingdom

Live Better Every Day!

Edited by Tony Watkins, MFA
Illustration by Michael Vilayvong
Vitruvian Man in Pentagon Logo Patent Pending

For information about permission to reproduce
selections from this book, write to:
Permissions, Full Life Balance Books and Seminars, LLC
P.O. Box 736
Fairfield, CA 94533

ISBN: 978-0-615-48128-9

FULL LIFE BALANCE BOOKS and SEMINARS, LLC
www.fulifebalance.com
William@fullcorporatetraining.com

FULL
life
BALANCE:
The 5 Keys to the Kingdom

"How to Live Better Every Day"

By

William K. Wesley, JD. MBA

TABLE OF CONTENTS

—

Acknowledgments

"The best things in life aren't things."-Anonymous

This book, these thoughts and feelings are dedicated to some of the "best things" in my life: to my life partner and wife, Linda, who helped save my life and replenishes it daily; to my late mother, Ora Campbell, who by her example showed me the minimum I was capable of; to the man who taught me how to be a man, my father, the late Mr. Bobbie Campbell; to my late grandmother, who just loved me, Mrs. Mittie (Gramon) Daniel; to my late grandfather, Mr. Robert Daniel (Jabo) — I kept on with my studies, just like you told me. Thank you. To my children, I hope I am showing you the minimum *you* are capable of: Tiye, William II and daughter-in-law Eva, Robert, Eunique and Rachael and son-in-law Aaron.

To my "baby sister" Shell, I pray you continue to stay the course. To my brother Dean, always remember you are us and we are you. To my brother Hugh, I hope something I have said or will say will help you "consider the possibilities" as you receive the many blessings I pray you continue to receive. To my brother James, I hope you see it is possible to consistently "do good and be good." To my sister Diane, hopefully you'll find something to help you with your journey.

To my grandchildren, you can stand on my head to reach anything, anytime: Jordan, Taja, Sydney, Aaron, Jr., Lauren and Ryan.

To my nieces and nephews, know your well runs deep.

To my friend and brother, Rev. Robert Duncan, we have inspired each other for most of our lives and I pray we continue. Thank you, thank you, thank you.

To my sisters- and brothers-in-law, thank you for sharing your lives and your hearts with my family.

To Eugene Chase, Jamal Gallow, Camara Rajabari, Eugene "Lou" Hall, Michael Allen, Dennis Roberts and Harold Brown, past and present friends— thank you.

To the author and friend who simply said, "Why don't you write a book?"—Pamela Ayo Yetunde, thanks again. It's amazing what one can do one page at a time.

And lastly, my defacto Full Life Balance "council:" Mr. Tony Watkins, MFA (editor); Ms. Mary Evans, JD; Dr. Fannie and Mr. Johnnie Preston; Mr. Carter Rankin; and my interns and students from Golden Gate University: Ruth Ann Aguliar, Nathaniel Hedges, and Nash Lundquist. Thank you all for your tireless work and support. Special thanks for dragging me into the social networking space.

—

How to Use This Book

Read it. Read it and review it. While reading it, if something resonates with you, if a suggestion makes sense to you — think it over and then...

Try it. If you develop any interest in the concepts at all, I suggest you try that concept for at least 90 days. From meditating daily to eating five smaller meals each day to playing the family game.

As long as it makes some sense to you, try it. What have you got to lose? As mental triggers, I summarize the secrets at the end of each chapter in order to make the suggestions and learnings flow into each other. When you are done with this book, if you find it was worth your time...

Pass it on. As you would do with anything of value, share it with your friends. Also, I would love to hear your thoughts, opinions and suggestions.

Write me at: **fulifebalance@yahoo.com**. See you at the end.

Prologue

I wrote *Full Life Balance: The Five Keys to the Kingdom* (FLB) as a testimony to the power of the spirit and family, and how managing the keys has helped my life. I believe striving for balance is something all can do. I do not contend to have *perfected* this in my life. Like most of us, I still have work to do. But, and I emphasize this, the journey to become balanced is what has helped me and will help you "Live Better Everyday" ®. *Full Life Balance: The Five Keys to the Kingdom* is my first book. I have developed seminars and workshops to support the concepts mentioned here.

I am a college professor, corporate trainer and author. I am a former retail store manager, financial advisor, investor education specialist, bank branch manager and vice-president of investor education for firms such as Morgan Stanley, Charles Schwab, Citibank and Merrill Lynch.

I am a former San Francisco Human Rights commissioner. As a non-profit board member, I have helped raise millions and have managed millions more for my investment clients. I have been recruited to sit on boards and committees, and I created a non-profit program to help youth. I hosted and produced my own television show. I have an MBA, a law degree (JD), and a list of licenses. I am a Dispute Resolution Arbitrator with the Financial Industry Regulatory Authority (FINRA), and I was the student commencement speaker of my graduating law class.

But this book is not about those accomplishments. It is about the course of my life, what I learned on the path I chose, and how what I learned will help you.

I wrote the majority of this book in 2001 and set it on the shelf after being accepted to law school. After experiencing many of life's spiritual, emotional, physical, professional and social successes and challenges over the years — including losing my mother to cancer, watching a son graduate from Berkeley and a daughter get her MBA, another daughter become a director at a Fortune 500 company, having a son go into the Navy to become a demolitions expert, watching two nephews go to prison, being laid off when my firm downsized, having my second spiritual epiphany, and graduating from law school — I picked up this manuscript in 2010 and decided to finish it.

It took about eight months to write this book, but the societal conditions and life events that led to this effort may go back hundreds, even thousands of years. Most of what's contained herein is my thoughts, observations and actual experiences. I have added additional stories, analogies, survey results, quotes, and sayings; not only to help make the reading more interesting, but to illustrate, highlight and/or reinforce certain points, observations or concepts. I am not an expert on life, love, diet, exercise, family or spirituality. I do, however, strive to be better in all of these areas everyday. I wrote this book because I am a thinking, feeling, and observant male human being of African descent.

Like most of my kind in America, my familial post-African origins date back to the slave-South. From there, like many others, my ancestors migrated to one of the major urban centers of this country. I am a first-generation, urban ghetto product from Hunters Point, San Francisco, CA. Hunters Point is a low-income, primarily blue-collar, high-crime, high-unemployment area located in the southeast section of San Francisco, with a high percentage of public housing.

—

9

The population is largely African American, but all cultures and races are represented. This type of urban environment represents the typical place of birth for many of those of African descent in America.

Raised with a spiritual base firmly rooted in the Baptist church, I learned of a jealous GOD who wanted our devotion in thought and deed. Without evidence of this devotion, which was to be demonstrated by following the Ten Commandments, one would surely die a lost soul, destined to burn in hellfire for eternity.

A product of the San Francisco public school system who ironically found himself temporarily subscribing to the philosophy of the Nation of Islam while pursuing my undergraduate degree at a private Jesuit university, I have traveled a very interesting but not that unique educational, political, physical, social and philosophical road which set the stage for the development of *Full Life Balance*.

I hope you are reading this because you are searching for something. I hope you have found your purpose, and this book will simply enhance your life. But if you are uncomfortable with your life and your prospects, I hope you find interesting answers and suggestions in these pages and are moved to achieve your complete, abundant destiny. I pray you find *Full Life Balance* as enlightening to read as I have found it to live and write.

Introduction

Let's go back to the early 1990's. My life was out of balance. I drank too much, I worked too much, I smoked, I used drugs, I watched too much TV, I ate the wrong amounts of the wrong things, I wasn't exercising, I wasn't reading, I wasn't learning anything new. I was depressed, I lied to myself and to others, and I felt anxious. I resented those whom I thought had less talent but were more successful than I financially, vocationally, and socially. I felt limited and frustrated in my career, and was a bad partner in a bad marriage with children I loved and cared about.

I knew, as a result of my upbringing, that there was a power or spirit greater than me, but I wasn't in contact with it. I wasn't praying or meditating, or even thinking there could be a spiritual or physical way out of the morass I was in. I had pretty much resigned myself to accept my confused, bored, lonely, envious and out-of-balance state. I just figured I would eat, drink, smoke, party, lie, work, and sleep for another thirty to forty years or so; and that, my friend, would simply be that.

But the curious piece of it all was I just didn't appear to be normal—I was normal. Compared to my friends, some of my family, co-workers, and most of the society I was in contact with and aware of, I *was* normal. Oh, I looked good, dressed well, made decent money; but inside, I was empty. Something was missing.

My turning point came in 1993. I had filed for divorce, my soon to be ex-wife had my three children, and I was taking life without my kids very hard. I was a store manager with a West Coast consumer electronics firm. I worked 45-55 hours per week, managed 35-40 people, and commuted two to three hours per day. After work, I would stop off and have at least one drink prior to driving home. Not wanting to go to my kid-less house, I would often grab a bite somewhere and then spend the remainder of the evening drinking, smoking, and partying until I felt "right" (or numb) enough to call it a day. I was miserable and getting progressively worse; but the drinks and the related mental clutter helped me pretend I was OK.

There was a new lady in my life, and I fed her lies (and I believed she believed them) about who I was, how good I was at what I did, and what I had. I didn't know at the time she had been placed in my life to help save me.

One night, after a particularly long yet uneventful repetition of the eating-driving-drinking-smoking routine, I arrived home at about two a.m. and was miserable. I felt lost, cold and disheartened. It seemed I was too old and too young and too tired and too empty — all at the same time. I was too old to be on the streets and in the clubs chasing what I was chasing. I was too young to be trapped in a life routine that might be essentially the same until I died. And I felt too drained and too dead emotionally, spiritually, and physically to do anything about it.

I went into my bedroom and thought maybe I should pray. I knelt by the bed in my fancy suit and realized I hadn't prayed in quite some time. And more alarming, I didn't know *what* to pray. I knelt there for a few awkward moments, and then I simply talked to GOD *the spirit*. I asked it to help me. I confessed that I was afraid of many things, one of which was ending up as the old guy in the club ("You're not too old, you're just too old to be here and doing that"). I apologized for

---

12

how I had treated my family and friends, and I asked for forgiveness. I asked for help. I admitted I could not do this by myself. I confessed that I was tired, scared, and did not know what to do to make myself better. I asked GOD to take away this appetite I had developed for wanting to numb myself everyday, and to replace it with an appetite for life.

As I continued to pray, I found myself talking out loud, begging and pleading with GOD to help me; and then something surprising happened: I began to cry. Not just tears, but real howling, wailing, crying. My chest heaved in and out and I bawled like a baby. I guess I was letting it all out. There must have been a lot in, because I was crying up a storm. After three? five? ten minutes? — I really don't know — I stopped, exhausted, and went to sleep fully-clothed on top of my bed.

I awoke the next day at about 8:00 a.m. and immediately knew something was different. I knew I would be all right. I felt different. I was comfortable. I knew I had been given a second chance. I felt I was all right. GOD, *the spirit* (whatever you call it — I don't think the name matters, but more on this later) touched me, and I responded to the power of the touch. I knew I would now be OK.

I was scheduled to arrive at work at 9:00 a.m. The store I managed was nearly two hours away. I called my boss to share and confess the agony I had been going through, and how different I was after the night of personal purging. He said to me, "I am glad you finally stepped up. I knew something like this was going on with you." (I found out later that he had gone through his own personal crisis and had also been rescued by *the spirit* and by others who cared about him. He had been watching me slowly self-destruct, and was torn about

---

13

how to reach out to me.) My manager told me he would have someone take care of the store, and literally ordered me to call the Employee Assistance Program and focus on taking care of myself. I called.

Two days later, I was heading for a 30-day life-changing experience at a recovery program in the Napa Valley. Nestled among rolling hills, wineries, and fresh air is an organization of incredible people who, in thirty days, helped me give me back to me.

When I woke up after the night of crying prayers, I knew I would be OK. While in St. Helena, I learned some of the initial steps of *how* to be OK. I took what I learned about needs, desires, insecurities, and addictive personalities, and began to rebuild my life. As I grew stronger in every sense of the word, I began to put together the essence of *Full Life Balance* in my daily life. Using my interpretation of spirituality as the foundation, I realized my life was better when I also acknowledged the needs of my physical, emotional, professional, and charitable self.

Over time, I truly fell in love with and then married the woman who stood by me during this awakening and the resulting life-reconstruction, began to give *quality* time to my children, resumed my formal academic career, developed my professional career, increased my volunteer activities (even created programs to help young people), began to read and learn again (for pleasure and for self-development), resumed playing the guitar, and began to play tennis nearly every week. In short, I began to live my life in a full and balanced way: I began to nurture my *spirituality*, pay attention to my *emotions*, positively address the *physical* part of me, develop my *professional* aspect, and resumed my *social* and *charitable* activity.

—

But the most telling effect of *Full Life Balance* is that for the first time in my adult life, I could say I was truly, truly at peace.

Ok, a little more background. My upbringing was on the surface a fairly common one for the majority of African American males in America. Low income, divorced parents, public housing, lots of fun and siblings, but limited resources pretty much paint the picture of my early childhood. By age ten, I had lived in five different places and attended five different elementary schools, but was having so much fun just *being* that I was virtually oblivious to my poverty and the reasons for my family's frequent relocations.

Around age ten was when the second biggest change of my life happened (the first was my parents' divorce when I was nine). My mother remarried. She married the late Mr. Bobbie Campbell, who would provide the daily example of what being a man was all about. Once Bobbie and Ora became one, they had a daughter, Donna. Now there were eight of us; and for the first time in our lives, we had stability.

Within three years, we had moved into the first house we had ever owned. I couldn't believe it. We had bought a house. Later, we bought a pool table, then a ping-pong table; and then we took a trip to Yosemite, and on and on. It was as if I had two separate childhoods. The first ten years of my life were full of financial problems, constant relocations, and the physical abuse of my mother by my biological father; the second ten were full of stability, plenty of food and toilet tissue, camps, vacations, and household peace. My dad, Mr. Bobbie Campbell, was the most stabilizing and behavior-modifying influence of my pre-teen life (outside of my mother's educational and social proddings).

15

I was clearly a man-child who responded better to a male figure than to a woman. In spite of how my biological father treated and abused my mother, I was still very attached to him. So, when I first met Mr. Bobbie Campbell, I hated him. He was organized, disciplined, self-actualized and he would quickly and specifically tell you what you needed to do, how to do it, why it needed to be done, and what would happen if the mission was not accomplished; but it was also very clear to us that he deeply loved, respected and enjoyed my mother. My siblings and I constantly tried to regurgitate the steady doses of punctuality, neatness and self-respect he tried to feed us. He had spent time as a drill sergeant during the Korean War and it initially appeared to us that he thought there was still a war on. There was: him against the Wesley children and their bad habits.

Don't get me wrong. My mother was doing an admirable job raising the five of us (at the time, four boys and a girl); but we lived in the Bayview Hunters Point area of San Francisco, were African American, and were surely going to need the advice, guidance and love from a strong, disciplined and self-aware male figure. This was especially important for me.

About now you may be asking yourself, so what happened? As I think you will see in the following pages, during my adolescent years I had a stable, loving, exciting, self-respecting, positive family. We went to church and believed what we learned. We were taught by example and by lecture to help our fellow man. We were taught to accept responsibility for our actions. We traveled modestly. We were taught manners. We were taught to try to do the right thing at home and in public. We believed we were organically equal to anyone who had ever drawn a breath. We were taught that the value of a person was not based on race, background,

---

educational or economic status; one's actions determined their value. I had a wonderful mother and exactly the father I needed to get me through those crucial teenage years.

So how did I end up in my late 30's miserable, without my children, prone on my bed in my suit, having the night of crying prayers? What went wrong? Could it have been avoided? The answer: I got out of balance. Not all at once. I can not point to a specific place and time and say, *that's* where it happened. I lived my life. I made some left turns and made some right turns. I made some wrong decisions and I made some right ones; but at almost every turn, I knew when I was doing the right thing just as clearly as *I knew when I was doing wrong*. All the while, through ins and outs and ups and downs, I realize now in hindsight that I was getting further and further out of balance. But the good news is: everything that happened to me from birth to the night of crying and the morning of epiphany led me to this exact point in the space-time continuum. I am here, writing this book, telling you that there is a way out, a better way, a way that is **Simple, Natural and Spiritual;** *and* **It Is All Connected**.

Several things I have learned on the journey may help to shed some light. I learned and now believe: 1) In the majority of cases, our parents and family are not responsible for how we end up. I was fed, loved, attended to and kept safe. The rest was and is still up to me. (However, had I been chained in a basement, abused, and whipped like a dog, well, the resulting faulty wiring from that abuse is well documented in our society. But that's the basis for an entirely different life and book.) The overwhelming majority of you reading this were loved, fed, attended to, and cared for by folks who did the best they could; so the person you now are as an adult is *a reflection* of your family. Still, it's primarily up to you. 2) People are incredibly strong. 3) We all have the ability to change. 4) We can always be more than we are.

What is *Full Life Balance*?

Full Life Balance (FLB) is a way to "Live Better Everyday" ®. A way to a life that is full, healthy, productive, purposeful, and exciting. FLB offers a guide to a better life by developing balance among our five natural needs and desires. As human beings, we are unavoidably inclined toward 1) spiritual contact (spiritual), 2) good health (physical), 3) emotional engagement (emotional), 4) personal achievement (professional), and 5) charitable activity (charitable).

The primary tenet of FLB is simply this: success can and will be achieved. Thus, the goal of FLB is to help you to take care of your most important asset – You. Take care of *your total self* in order to live a full, healthy, productive, purposeful and exciting life.

Why should I journey this way to a *Fully Balanced Life*?

Have you been searching? Do you wonder what "it" is all about? Have you ever defined success as the glamour of having all the money and possessions you ever dreamed of? Did you believe that by achieving "success" you would find happiness and contentment?

Now that you are "successful" and have acquired all the material things in your wildest dreams, *are you happy? Do you feel contentment?* Do your children know what you believe in, what your principles are, and what you stand for? Do *you* show the world what *you* believe in, what your principles are, and what you stand for?

Or, are you a person you never imagined you would be? Do you find yourself wondering, "When will it be my turn? Why can't I have the things I want? Why *not* me?" Do you drink or smoke too much, eat heavily, lose yourself in front of your TV or computer, or let yourself be consumed by work? Do you experience one bad relationship after another? Can't sleep at night, worry too much, live in boredom, or feel just plain *hopeless*? Do you feel that you should be doing, feeling, and *living better* - but just can't figure out *how*? Do these questions haunt you?

Or, are you just starting out in life and career? Are you asking yourself, "How can I avoid or minimize the pitfalls that I see so many others make?" Do you wonder how you can craft your path?

Well, *Full Life Balance* is the answer. *Full Life Balance* will show you how to harness the power of *the spirit* from within. With that, you will be able to harness the power of the universe. You can and *will* be better, happy, in love, and healthier. You will have what you truly and naturally need and desire. You can live well. If you commit to the process, this can and will happen for you. You are the best judge of FLB's effectiveness, but others will also evaluate your growth.

So, that's what FLB is. Here's what FLB is not. It is not a pill; it is not a quick cure; it does not cost money. The results are *guaranteed not* to be the same for

19

everyone, but results are guaranteed for those who are willing to seek their *Full Life Balanced* self. It will not work unless you work at it. FLB is not based on race or religion or income or sex or sexual preference. It is not an answer that lies on the outside of you and no one can do it for you. You can begin but it does not have an end point. The goal is to achieve success through the process.

How was *Full Life Balance* developed?

Full Life Balance began for me as a **spiritual awakening** and then blossomed to encompass all aspects of my being: the physical, emotional, professional, and charitable facets of my life. As a result, I was inspired to write this book in order to shed some light on the process which has allowed me to change *my* life and positively affect the lives of those around me. This is not an empirical, analytical, or clinical study; this is simply what happened to me, and how I now live my life as a result. It is a guideline; not the only one, but one I *know* works.

The idea of *Full Life Balance* has existed for years and years in one form or another. Many people have achieved what I am in the process of achieving. Many continue to search for their answer, their key — the vehicle or method or process whereby they begin to understand and truly enjoy themselves and others, and find what life is all about. There have been numerous books and articles written on the subject, many of them quite good. Many seminars and workshops have been created in an attempt to guide the willing along the path.

However, I have found that many works on this subject do a good job addressing the non-spiritual aspects, but often give minimal treatment to the spiritual facet of a *fully balanced life*. Others spend ample time on the importance of one's spiritual self, but fall short when it comes to physical, emotional, professional and charitable "health." I believe the most important aspect of one's self is the spiritual; however, to completely enjoy *Full Life Balance*, one must develop and grow in all areas of life. Once you achieve balance in spirit, it can flow to all aspects of your existence. However, this flow has to be channeled, guided, and directed to facilitate the full awareness and maximum useful, enjoyable and healthy effect.

Too often we encounter those who appear very religious or spiritual, but who are also unhealthy, overweight, and out of shape. We encounter those who have the material toys and trinkets, but have literally lost their souls in the rush to accumulate. We encounter others who flutter in the middle — unsure, unfocused, unfulfilled, and unable to share in the bounty of life. *Full Life Balance is the answer.*

Over the years, I've given presentations at churches and other organizations on this incredible *fully balanced life* I am now living, developing and evolving. I have received enthusiastic endorsements from attendees as to how my discussion of *Full Life Balance* has enhanced their lives.

So one day, I thought, "I should write all of this down." That thought, coupled with the suggestion from a friend to "Just write it and let an editor edit it," helped this lifestyle become the book you now hold in your hands.

First Things First

My dad, Mr. Bobbie Campbell, said to me, "ninety-nine percent of the things that happen to you happen because you allow them, or because you cause them. The rest is good or bad luck." The longer I live, the truer these words ring. However, I am not discounting the evil and biases interwoven into the fabric of human history. Man's inhumanity to man existed long before you and I came here, and will surely outlive us. What I am saying and do believe is, to paraphrase my dad, we are directly responsible for the overwhelming majority of things that happen to us. I believe the acceptance of personal responsibility for yourself and your actions is the essential prerequisite for personal development and change. I believe if you can grow and develop as an individual, you will become a better family member; and better family members make better families and better families make better communities, and on and on. In sum, you are the *primary* agent of change in your circumstance, and you can change the world.

The Kinghood and Queenhood

From the beginning of time, all children have needed role models and discipline to help them learn, identify, and respect the boundaries of socially acceptable behavior; especially the biggest and strongest (the males). If young males perceive themselves as the biggest and strongest creatures in their world without learning by example, from adult males, how to behave as the biggest and strongest, then they become key ingredients in a recipe for societal failure.

The *American Heritage Dictionary* defines a "king" as "one that is preeminent in a group, category or sphere"; "queen" as "…eminent or supreme in a given domain and personified by a woman; and "hood" as a "condition, state, (or) quality." From these definitions we have the terms "Kinghood" and "Queenhood." I define them both as achieving or attaining the condition of spiritual, emotional, professional, social and actual preeminence in one's group, family, community, country, and/or race. (NOTE: For ease of reading, I will most often use the term Kinghood to encompass both concepts.)

I found a great example to illustrate the importance of adult males carrying the mantle of Kinghood in a society. This story has an eerie parallel to what *always* occurs among humans. This particular society happened to be in the animal kingdom, but the parallels were too incredibly similar not to include here.

I was watching one of the nature shows recently. The caretakers of a wildlife preserve in Africa sent out a call for help from African elephant and rhinoceros experts. They had a serious problem. Groups of young bull elephants were harassing, attacking, injuring, and even killing the rhinoceros, without apparent provocation. None of the experts had ever experienced such aggressive group behavior (reminiscent of human juvenile gangs) on the part of elephants.

The experts considered the possible causes one by one: territorial disputes, musk-induced aggression, perceived or real threats to the very young, and the like. All agreed: none of these possible provocations were the cause. The scientists then turned their attention to the origins of the specific herd of elephants. They had been transferred from another preserve as a group, but only pre-teen and teenage male elephants had been transferred. No mature adult males had made the journey.

Further observation led the scientists to the following conclusion: **Without adult males as role models and to provide normal discipline, the adolescent males had become juvenile delinquents**. The juvenile elephants didn't have the behavior of an adult bull to emulate; therefore, *any* behavior they, the juveniles, *deemed* acceptable *became* acceptable behavior. They didn't have the bulls to discipline them; therefore, they could get anyway with anything. They were the biggest and strongest creatures in their world — who could stop them? They had only themselves and other misguided teenagers to use as barometers of behavior.

In animal and human societies, similar examples can be found to demonstrate the effect the absence of females as disciplinarians and role models has on the family and culture. In general, youth of all species will emulate the most influential figures around them. Human history and the human present make one conclusion exceedingly clear: more men and women must develop into the state of Kinghood and Queenhood in order to become the positive examples many young people will want to imitate.

What are some of the signs you have reached Kinghood? When your parents look to you for advice; when your children quote you (out loud; or, as with many adolescent children, in thought evidenced by action) as a reliable source; when your grandparents say you "turned out nice;" when more good people like you than dislike you; when your parents ask you to help someone "straighten out their life;" when even those who don't like you still respect you; when you look in your mirror and can honestly say, "I am glad to be who I am."

There are literally millions of men and women who exist in the state of Kinghood. Our society desperately needs more. Single-parent families, gay families, those families without direct responsibilities for children, single people — there is no social prerequisite for Kinghood. Men and women who embrace this attribute and develop their roles in society are better men and women, regardless of their origin. History shows us that better men and women help to make better families, and better families help to make better societies. If you are living in Kinghood, those who come in contact with you will know that you are a positive, self-aware individual. Your actions as a result will positively affect the world. It is time for Kinghood.

Take the hypothetical example of the child not of African descent who is raised by a man of African descent who is embracing his Kinghood. That child's perception of those of African descent — and Kinghood — will be shaped and enhanced by the contact with the man who raised that child and interacted with that child's mother. If that man is living in Kinghood, there is a very good chance that the child will have a healthy, positive view of men in general and men of African descent in particular. There is also a very good chance that the child will imitate the behavior present in the home. Further, the man becomes a role model for that child's friends to emulate as they mature. Society wins when men live in Kinghood.

I am not saying everything and everyone connected to you will turn out well because you live seeking FLB and Kinghood. I am saying that you will increase the odds of good positive behavior if you are an example of it. Love starts at home; so does ignorance, which I believe is the primary breeder of hate and racism. What a child is taught at home through word and deed, that child will take into the world. Who knows what potential that child's life holds, and what changes that child is destined to bring to the world?

I often speak about the need for men to stand in Kinghood. But, Kinghood and *Full Life Balance* are not about male or female, black, red, yellow, or white, Christian or Muslim or Jew, straight or gay, married or single; it is about self-actualization for all people. It is about striving relentlessly to live a full, abundant and balanced life.

However, being male and acutely aware of the numbers of men in prison and being sentient of the amount of violence, injustice, abuse, neglect perpetrated by men against men, women and children versus the relatively small numbers of women guilty of the same infractions, a major part of my focus in this book is on men, for the men themselves and all of those connected to them. FLB and an understanding of Kinghood will help everyone who embraces and actively pursues the concepts.

One last thing: While you are reading, if I say anything that makes sense for you and your family, I challenge you to make notes about how FLB could affect your life. When you are finished, I challenge you to make a list of the activities that you will do for 90 days in order to achieve FLB. I have included a questionnaire for you to use. And finally, I ask that you contact me after the initial reading and then again after 90 days to share your story with me.

Ok, now on to *Full Life Balance: The Five Keys to the Kingdom.*

IT IS SIMPLE, IT IS NATURAL AND IT IS ALL CONNECTED

The Five Precepts of Full Life Balance:

1. There is a spirit that keeps the universe in spiritual and physical balance.

2. The universal law of cause and effect is true for all things.

3. We are spiritual beings having a physical experience.

4. Most things have essentially happened before, but nothing can be done the exact same way twice. Everything one does is individual and unique to the existence of the human race; therefore: You are the one, I am the one.

5. Thought is the first physical action.

THE FIVE KEYS OF FULL LIFE BALANCE

The Physical Key

"You can't plow a field by turning it over in your mind."- Anonymous
"To keep a lamp burning we have to keep putting oil in it."- Mother Teresa.

The Basics. Amazing things happen to us when we attain the correct balance of the basics: diet, rest, water, exercise, and prevention. If life requires energy, *Full Life Balance* requires megawatts of it. To live a full, balanced life, a life that includes family, friends, exercise, a career, social and charitable activities, you must have sustained energy. On this road to *Full Life Balance,* I have found certain activities work well for me. By "work well," I mean they help develop, strengthen, and rejuvenate my body and my mind. I have also found it important to develop physical, mental and cultural hobbies just for the fun of it. If something is enjoyable, I tend to want to do it again. How about you? Also, in order to enjoy things in life you have to be *alive.* So I have included some additional thoughts on survival instincts.

Diet, rest, water, exercise and prevention. As of this writing, I have missed only a few days of work due to illness since April of 1994. I think it is due in large part to the fact that I practice *Full Life Balance.* I am one of the busiest people I know. I have children and I speak in person to groups of people for a living, so I am exposed to as many, if not more, communicable diseases as you or any other normal person. But once I started living a full and balanced lifestyle, my immune system developed to the point where I might have occasional sniffles or cough; but the flu, colds, and other diseases that plague many people on a seasonal basis haven't stopped at my doorstep in years.

For what it's worth, here are some of my habits. I eat four to five times per day. I sleep as soundly as a baby and often take a couple of 20- to 30-minute naps per week. I do some type of exercise every day, participate in a strenuous physical sport twice weekly, and have a physical check-up roughly every 12 to 18 months. Let's look at how I balance each of the physical basics.

Diet. Many dietary experts suggest you should eat 4 to 5 small meals per day. They contend that it is not only healthier for you and better for your digestive system, but that it allows you to have a more constant and sustained level of energy. I agree with that contention and am living proof that it works. In addition, almost all of the things your mother probably told you about what to eat are essentially true.

My mom taught us the value of the proper foods. For example, we were eating wheat bread in the early 1960's. By the way, as children, my siblings and I wanted white bread like other kids and Wonder Bread ® television commercials said we should. Even though our mother explained the nutritional benefits of wheat bread, we always thought we were being deprived of something good. As we grew in knowledge and in age, we obviously began to not only see but also appreciate Mom's ahead-of-the-curve health knowledge and practices. (Thanks, Mom☺.)

Frequent daily servings of fruit, vegetables, breads, cereals, nuts, poultry, fish, rice or potatoes and a little red meat (once a week or so) are good for most folks. Of course, I am not a dietary expert; and if am suggesting anything contrary to what your dietitian has described, please, by all means follow the advice of the expert who knows your particular circumstance.

I don't suggest this is a perfect diet, but I do know that it has served me extremely well for many years. Also, since I am in balance (that is, I don't consciously pollute my body with destructive substances such as tobacco or drugs); I tend to eat what I naturally feel like eating. Therefore, my diet is not as rigid as it appears. My body tells me what it needs, and I feed it. When I am thirsty, I drink. When I am hungry, I eat. When I want sugar, I have something sweet—cake, cookies, energy bar, yogurt, or candy. When I want something salty, I buy a bag of chips or pretzels. These are things that my body wants occasionally; because I strive to maintain balance, I don't feel the need or desire to consume a quart of ice cream or the family-pack of potato chips by myself in one sitting.

Consult with your doctor, books, magazines, and the web to find the food combinations that work best for you. For those of you with restrictive conditions, I want to stress again, make sure you consult with a professional who *is familiar with your circumstance.*

Most folks can probably do what I do. Simply, find out what's good for your body; find out how much of it you need; then eat the right amount of it, spread over the right time frame, with the correct frequency. In diet, as with nearly all things, moderation is paramount.

One day, I acted as chaperone as my youngest daughter's class went on a field trip to a farm. I noticed an approximately foot-long, foot-wide block of salt hanging on a post near where the cows grazed. I learned that occasionally a cow will walk over to the salt-lick and actually lick it a few times. The cow will not gnaw at it to the point of developing a disease such as high-blood pressure. The cow (or any animal) will only satisfy its natural, biological need.

Humans are the only species known to man that will willfully and deliberately consume products that are physically harmful and in deleterious amounts. Legal drugs such as tobacco and hard alcohol are perfect examples, not to mention the illegal ones. This conscious consumption of destructive substances (and the over-consumption of non-destructive substances, i.e., eating too much and the eating the wrong foods) may be caused not only by being out of balance in one's diet, but by being out of balance in one's life as well.

Tips on eating: eat until you are comfortable, not full; only eat when you are hungry, not because the food is there; if you don't like something, don't continue to eat it, but use that hunger instead on something you enjoy and that is good for you. There are plenty of good-tasting, good-for-you foods. Don't eat late night, and don't get up to eat midnight snacks; and drink a glass of water first thing in the morning and one about 90 minutes before you go to bed.

31

Rest. All living things need rest in order to replenish their bodies. My career requires, among other responsibilities, that I fly to different cities to give presentations. Every time I return, one of the first calls I make is to my grandmother (Hi, Gramon☺). One of the last things she says to me after we talk briefly about my trip is, "I know you are tired. Go home and get some rest." It seems that all of my adult life, my grandmother has been asking me if I want something to eat and telling me to go and get some rest. Over the years, she has helped me learn the value of two of the most important things a body needs: rest and food. Even in FLB, I am a naturally busy, somewhat compulsive multi-tasking person, who still has room for improvement when it comes to getting rest and not over-working.

I have come to understand the value of, and grown to appreciate, how a nap can rejuvenate. I always thought a nap was for babies and old people. Maybe it is. Maybe I turned old and didn't know it. All I know is, now, after a busy day at work and before an evening presentation, I will often take a 20- to 30-minute nap before going to do the event. It helps me stay charged, fresh, and ready to go.

I treasure the time I have to sleep, and try to make sure nothing interferes with that time. I also try to be in the correct mental state for peaceful sleep. Part of the correct mental state for sleep is to simply accept and realize that there is little else you can do about whatever happened today. It is over. Whether it was good or bad — it is over. Reflect on it, learn from it, and then get over it. And get some rest. Because if you are one of the "lucky" ones, you'll get another chance at it tomorrow. As Gramon might say, "You are going to need your strength." Good night.

———

In addition to rapid eye movement (R.E.M.) sleep—the good, deep sleep when the body does most of its restoring, repairing and replenishing—just lounging with a good book or favorite television show, sitting down, meditating, and lying down are all good ways to rest the body and mind.

In order to stay fresh, I try to get the correct amount of sleep, rest, and meditation for my mind and body. I have also learned that once every couple of months or so, I need to stay inside all day, in my pajamas, watching cartoons, reading an entertaining book, and snacking and drinking water and fruit juice all day. It's as if I am a car. I need periodic servicing; but instead of every several thousand miles, it's every few months.

In addition to the rest habits and rituals mentioned above, we also need a periodic extended break—a vacation. I'm probably the last person to advise you to take a vacation. Apparently, if it were up to me to plan it, I would rarely take one. I am lucky to have Linda in my life to help me with this extended rest requirement. A couple of years ago when I began the pursuit of my MBA, Linda suggested we should do something special when I graduated. At first I resisted, for no apparent reason. After some reflection, I realized that *we* would need an extended break. I worked full-time (with out-of-town travel nearly every month), was a fiancé and father, went to school, directed my non-profit youth organization, and played tennis almost weekly. Linda worked full-time, was a mother and full-time homemaker, sat on a board, *and* put up with me. We decided on a cruise to the Caribbean and set it for a couple months after I was scheduled to graduate. The time spent obtaining my MBA was one of the busiest of my life, and the time literally flew by.

Before I knew it, I was graduating and then packing for the islands. It was a great trip, with many beautiful sights coupled with exciting and fun memories. Those of you who have been to the islands know what I mean. For those who haven't been, go; it's worth it. In addition to the lasting memories of the beauty, the fun, and the people, one of my most interesting discoveries was how long it took for me to *truly* relax.

I rarely feel uptight, harried or stressed. I didn't feel some huge, overwhelming need physically or psychologically to take a vacation. But it took a couple of days before I stopped feeling that I had *something else* to do.

Here's what happened. After the first day of flying, gathering our bags, loading onto the ship, and then setting sail, we ate a wonderful dinner, hung out around the pool, listened to reggae music, and then just crashed. Overnight, the ship sailed to our first destination, St. Thomas. We toured the island and shops, and had a fun-filled time. We spent the next day at sea. About mid-day, I went to the pool area, selected a recliner, and reclined. This was my first extended period without any specific activity on the docket.

As I sat there, I just couldn't shake the nagging feeling that I had something to do or somewhere to go. You know what? I didn't. I had nothing to do and nowhere else to go. I was on a ship in the Caribbean, on vacation. Where else could I go?

Apparently, I was somewhat relaxed, but not completely. It actually took nearly two days for me to shake the feeling that there was something on my calendar which I had to attend to. Luckily for me, it was an 8-day cruise; because before I could totally shut down my engines, two of those days had blown by. I'm not saying I didn't have fun those first two days; I did. I just know I enjoyed myself more and was more enjoyable to be around after I totally relaxed. I took the time to reflect on the prior two years. I gained a greater appreciation for my accomplishments: MBA with honors, engagement, new job, and community work. I thanked God for giving me the ability to achieve what I had achieved, I patted myself on the back for a job well done, and realized that there was nothing else to do now but relax. I then *relaxed* and really began to enjoy the remainder of my vacation.

Sometimes you have stress but you can't feel it. Sometimes you just need to force yourself to take an extended break, and consciously let it all hang out. Sometimes you need to give yourself permission to relax and celebrate a job well done. My trip was absolutely incredible. And replenishing. Once I got into the right mental space, my big decisions became, "Do I order steak or lobster for dinner? Steak *or* lobster? Give me steak *and* lobster!" I lounged, I played, I laughed; and I loved it. It was great.

Water. You are mostly water. One of things you need most is water. After air and right before food on the scale of what our bodies need to survive, is water. The general consensus among health professionals is that we need somewhere between six to eight twelve-ounce glasses of the elixir of life per normal day. More if you are outside in hot weather or participating in strenuous activity. Gramon used to always tell us to make sure we drank plenty of water. That's all I have to say about that.

Exercise. I play tennis nearly every week. I jokingly refer to it as my therapy. In order to play tennis, I have to keep myself in shape. I spend five minutes stretching from head to toe, and I do push-ups and sit-ups most mornings. Occasionally, I ride my stationary bike and/or do a light weight workout. This routine gives me the strength, flexibility, and stamina to participate vigorously in the physical hobby I enjoy.

Most days, I drive to BART, our local mass transit system; park anywhere from 1 to 8 blocks away; and walk to the station. Once there, I walk down the stairs rather than take the elevator or escalator; stand instead of sit; and read a book while waiting for the train. When I get off the train, I walk up the three flights of stairs and then a block to my office. During the day, I take at least three walks, and stretch often. The simple point here is, in order to stay in shape and active, *one must move on a regular basis.* If you work in an environment where movement is difficult, figure out a way to do periodic daily physical activity. If you have to sit for long periods of time, stand up and stretch, do a few deep knee bends every fifteen minutes or so, contract a muscle in a different region of your body every five minutes for a thirty minute period, then repeat throughout the day. The list goes on and on. Make up your own exercises.

We have just got to exercise in order to become and stay healthy.

Most exercise professionals suggest that we get at least 25 minutes of cardio-pumping exercise every day. Jog, ride a bike, walk at a very brisk pace, swim, play basketball, play tennis, use a treadmill, use a Stairmaster ® — anything that gets your heart pumping rapidly for at least 25 minutes is helpful to the body. Just be sure to consult your doctor about your particular circumstance and ability.

Prevention. Diet, rest, water, and exercise are all part of the proactive preventive process. In addition, prevention includes regular check-ups, screenings, and visits to health care professionals when something is not quite right. While I was in my mid-thirties, my dad passed due to cancer. He was only 56 years old. Over the three-year period during which the illness took its toll and finally his life, I learned a lot about cancer. I learned there are different types. I learned about how cancer can be caused by external and internal forces. I also learned that there are certain key regions of the body that have a greater propensity for the disease (e.g., breast, lung, prostate). And I discovered certain people are genetically, environmentally, or otherwise predisposed to cancer (smokers; heavy drinkers; or even African American males in Washington, D.C., and San Francisco, who have a higher than normal incidence of prostate cancer).

However, I believe that the most important thing that I found out about cancer was that the possibility of contracting it can be greatly reduced by taking certain precautions or eliminating certain behaviors, and that it can often be successfully treated if diagnosed early enough. By the way, my dad's cancer was apparently genetic.

———

37

I decided, after watching him go through a horrid death, that when I turned forty I would begin having regular prostate exams. Well, that was much easier said than done. Ages 40, 41, and 42 came and went, and still no exams. I had physical check-ups, but no prostate exam. I talked to my friends; they all knew they should have the exam, too, but were hesitant. Were they afraid? Too self-conscious? Too embarrassed to let someone touch them *that* way? Well, apparently, so was I. It was one of the most ridiculous self-realizations I had ever made. Being African American, male, and living in San Francisco, I had classic high-risk factors for a disease that could cause a dreadful and often unnecessary death; but it also had a high survival rate if doctors identified the condition early enough. And *I* would not go to the doctor because I didn't want anyone to touch me *like that*. Well, the good news is: I finally went in.

The year I turned forty-three, I had the exam. It was performed by a man. He sensed the mental anguish I was going through; he even made a joke about being sorry that he wasn't going to buy me dinner afterwards. No cancer was found. I now go every year. Hey, guys, the first time is the worst; and that's *only* in your mind. After the first exam, it's a piece of cake. I've told all of my friends and family. Some of them have even had the exam recently.

When it's time to die, it's time to die; but whatever you can do to extend the time you have to live, you have just got to do it. We must take the preventive steps to guarantee that we don't pass on from illness that could have been treated and cured if found in time. And please do not let things as petty as ego, irrational ideas, or false beliefs get in the way of your regular and complete health maintenance routine. Get yourself fully checked out at least every two years.

Self-preservation and survival instincts. Another important aspect of the physical key is our natural desire for self-preservation or survival. All living things have a basic craving to continue living. In man as in other animals, the survival instinct is clearly the strongest. Over time, various animals have evolved different methods to assist in the survival of their kind: giraffes developed long necks to reach choice vegetation and to identify threats from afar; in addition to being fleet of foot, rabbits developed keen senses of smell and hearing to offset the lack of defensive physical strength; and cheetahs evolved into the fastest thing on two or four feet in order to ensure their ability to overtake one of the staples of their diet, the speedy Thompsons Gazelle.

In addition to easily-identifiable physical self-preservation characteristics, it is widely believed that most animals have some type of mechanism that allows them to sense the presence of danger. Generally, before they can even smell or see or hear an immediate threat, many animals in the wild will become more tense and alert. They actually feel or sense that there is a threat nearby.

In humans, this sense that allows us to feel that there might by danger lurking is often referred to as "a funny feeling," "a hunch," "my first mind," and other descriptions. The difference between humans and animals in regard to this sense (I refer to it as my Spider-sense from the old Spider-Man® comic books) is that we humans have the ability to override the warning that the sense is trying to convey. You may rationalize or talk yourself out of heeding the survival advice your physical self gives you. You may often discount and dismiss these feelings or messages by saying that you are just being silly and that everything will be just fine. But sometimes you may talk yourself out of safety and into trouble.

You might remember this story. A few years ago, a woman was jogging at dusk in a local park. It was beginning to get dark when she began having a weird feeling. She wanted to complete her workout, but she had a feeling that something just wasn't right and that maybe she should turn around and head back to her car. She quickly rationalized that feeling away and convinced herself that everything was fine. Moments later, she was attacked and brutally raped. Luckily she lived to tell the story.

A few years prior to this event, a young man graduated from college with an undergraduate degree in business. He had studied hard beside some of the best and brightest, and he had held his own. He was the first among his siblings to graduate from college. He had worked either part- or full-time during those years, and the self-discipline and confidence he had developed assured him that there "Ain't No Stoppin' Us Now." He was ready to live the title of his graduation party song. He was young, gifted, and black in America. He felt that the world was his oyster. It was his time. He felt he was as good as anyone, and was ready to go out into the world and make his fortune.

As a graduation present, his family decided to send him on a cross-country trip. His final vacation destination was Paradise Island in the Bahamas. He would take a 30-day bus ride across the lower half of America so that he could taste, touch, and feel his country. He was scheduled to arrive in Miami on the thirty-first day for an early flight to the Bahamas.

Before beginning his trip, his mother had pulled him aside and shared her heart-felt thoughts with him. She told him that she had raised him to believe that he could do anything and everything he put himself into. But she counseled him, "You were raised in Northern California, and you are about to go not just to the south, but the Deep South." She told him that things were different in the south, and that he would need to be careful and be aware. Out of respect and manners, he, of course, politely listened to and acknowledged his mother's words, all the while thinking, "What is she talking about? I can handle myself. I come from Hunters Point, California, where we 'Deal wit' it'."

Roughly two-thirds of the way into his trip, the young man found himself on a Greyhound bus pulling into Biloxi, Mississippi, about as Deep South as you can get. He had just spent the last twenty or so days of his fantastic voyage seeing and experiencing the sights and sounds of American life, from Los Angeles to Las Vegas to Phoenix to El Paso/Juarez to Dallas to New Orleans; and now he was in the bus depot in Biloxi. He checked his schedule; it showed that he had a two-hour layover. He checked his watch; it showed five-thirty. He checked his stomach; by the way it was growling, it showed it was hungry.

Most bus stations look the same, feel the same, and are located in the same section of town: run-down but being redeveloped, or just run-down. In Biloxi, the station was a decent one. While standing there, trying to decide what to eat, he felt something strange, something he just couldn't put his finger on. Something just didn't feel right. He asked someone in the bus station where he could find a good burger, got the answer, and headed out the door and down the humid Biloxi Street towards a greasy spoon about a block away.

41

It felt as thick as a blanket when he walked in. He couldn't see it, but apparently most of the patrons in the diner could; because nearly everyone in the dive turned and looked at him when he walked in. It was the same feeling he'd had in the bus station, but now it was worse. It was much, much worse. His Spider-sense was tingling. He felt like he was in one of those movies where the guy walks into a bar and the music stops, everyone stops talking, and just looks at him. He felt like he was in danger. He felt like he had just walked into a Klan diner where everyone in town, both black and white, knew who was not welcome there — everyone, that is, except him. And they were looking at him as if to say, "How dare you come in here, boy."

So now he's thinking, "Do I just turn and run — no, *walk* out of here? Do I grab a seat, sit down, and order a burger?" For some reason, he could almost hear the warning from his mother to be careful and aware. He accepts the fact that he is in a different place and that his life may be in danger, so the most important thing to do is to get back to the bus station in one piece. The other part of his mind says, "Don't show these clowns any fear." Still another part of his mind is saying, "I am a customer with money to spend. I can spend it anyplace I want." These thoughts are racing through his mind as he walks to the counter, with most of the folks in the place still staring at him. He says, "May I have a Coke to go, please?" The counter person doesn't reply; instead, she just walks to get the can of Coke, returns, sets it on the counter, and then looks at him.

He extends a dollar bill. She looks at it, and he knows instantly that she's not going to put her hand near his. So he sets the bill on the counter. She picks it up, makes change, and sets it on the counter. He picks up the change and the Coke, all in slow motion, all

———

42

under observation. He walks to the door, wondering if he'll get jumped and who will help him if he does. He closes the door behind him, takes a few steps, and then runs to the bus station. He glances back, hoping no one is following him. His hope is realized.

He makes it safely to the bus station. As he sits in a plastic molded, coin-operated TV-seat, all manner of thoughts cross his mind. He realizes that although he is an American and should be able to sit and eat at any public establishment, his Spider-sense had told him that it would have been unwise to sit and eat in *that* diner. His heart is pumping; his adrenaline-infused body is twitching. He thinks of the three voter registration workers and the night of terror that ended their young lives not too far from here some years ago. He thinks of Rev. Dr. Martin Luther King's "I Have Been to The Mountain Top" speech the night before he was assassinated. He thinks of unsolved lynchings, and he remembers the picture he's seen of a Klan "picnic." You know the picture, the one where a bunch of good old boys and their families, including children, are posing and smiling in front of tree that just happens to have the dead, mutilated body of someone who looks like our recent college graduate hanging from it. He is terrified. He is alone. He keeps watching the door, expecting them to come in and attack him. He keeps watching the clock, willing it to record his liberation from this home of southern hospitality in nanoseconds. He thinks, "I'm glad I didn't sit down to eat. I'm glad I remembered what my Mom said, and I'm glad I paid attention to my feelings." When he realizes that he is finally safe, he calms down and thinks in disgust, "Boy, *this* is the country I live in."

That young man was obviously me. I don't know if my Spider-sense saved my life that night, but I do know I clearly *felt* that I was in serious danger before I *saw* the signs and faces of the potential threat.

These are two examples of the need to heed the natural alarm. Don't overlook it; don't talk yourself out of it. Listen to it. Nurture it. It could save your life. Pay attention to it.

Physical hobbies. Physical hobbies are the sports and physical activities you enjoy. Exercise allows you to maintain a body that allows you to vigorously participate in your chosen physical hobbies. Let me paint the picture of what's happening with me right now, as I write this section. I just hopped out of the shower. It's about seven-thirty in the evening. I have had a full and exciting day at work. I feel high. I am listening to Thelonius Monk's *Best of* CD. I'm at my laptop, and I just feel good. After work, I played two sets of tennis. (By the way, I won 6-3, 6-3.) I played for nearly two hours. During that time, the most important things in the world to me were my serve, backhand, forehand, and footwork. I worked up a great sweat and my endorphins really kicked in. I am a fair tennis player, but every now and then I move my feet just right, turn my shoulders and hips just right, and hit a killer forehand or backhand, and I imagine I'm Arthur Ashe at Wimbledon in the mid-1970's, teaching the then-young upstart Jimmy Connors a lesson.

For me, it's one of the greatest feelings on earth. I plan to play tennis as long as I can walk, as long as I can breathe, as long as I can hold a racquet. As I write this, I am nearly 47 years old. I play against people older, younger, and the same age as me. Some play better than I do, some not as well. When I was 44, I was beaten pitifully by a 63-year-old-man. The gentleman walked with a limp, and I thought for sure I was going to run him off the court. He had me running all over the place and he seemed to barely break a sweat. He taught me tennis patience and humility on the court (I'm not claiming to have learned those lessons completely).

Last week I beat, just barely, a man 27 years of age. I think I might be helping him learn patience and humility. I have several different players in my personal rotation, and I play about forty-five weeks per year, often twice per week.

What does playing tennis have to do with *Full Life Balance*? Everything and possibly nothing. Everything for me, because tennis satisfies the need I have for a physical hobby. For you, possibly nothing. Tennis could be your least favorite sport on the planet. For you, it could be walking, cycling, rowing, jogging, basketball. The key is to actively participate in any *active endorphin-releasing sport*.

The point is simple: in order to live a *Full Balanced Life*, one must do some physical activity that gets the heart pumping, the blood racing, the lungs bellowing, and the brain releasing endorphins.

Do you remember how you felt when you were a kid? If you were lucky like me, most of your days were spent running, jumping, laughing, playing, fantasizing — in general, just enjoying being a kid. Of course, there were school, chores and such; but the feeling I remember was being on a type of high most of the time. Unknown to most of us then, our running and playing and fantasizing all helped to trigger the release of hormones that made us feel good. Those mechanisms and feelings are still with and available to you. Use them, but trigger them and use them in a healthy manner.

The health benefits of physical activity have been well-documented. Physically, mentally, and emotionally, you gain if you engage in regular physical activity. Your body becomes healthier and stronger, your mind becomes clearer and sharper, and the release you get from exercise helps your emotional state.

But that's only half the story. It's also fun. It fills a competitive need. It fills a need for physical accomplishment. You can become proficient, if not good, at almost any activity that you give the required practice. And as you work at your chosen activity, you lose sight of yourself; you lose touch with the good and bad of the day. Almost everything else becomes insignificant when you begin to put yourself totally into the activity; and therein lies the release of stress and anxiety. I am not saying to drop this book and, without the requisite training, go run a marathon. I am advocating a regimen that allows you to build up the necessary stamina and skill (if required) to actively and regularly participate in an activity that gets your juices flowing. The hidden benefit is the fact that action creates the ability for more action. Physical activity drains us in the short term while increasing our stamina and ability in the long term.

Mental hobbies. Just as you exercise your body, you should also enjoy exercising your mind. Video games, chess, cards, dominoes, writing, television game shows that force you to think, reading, puzzles, model airplanes, collectibles — whatever, as long as it's something enjoyable and it requires you to think (process, calculate, recall, speculate, analyze, conclude) while doing it. The mental hobbies I enjoy most are teaching, lecturing, reading, and playing chess. I read one to two books per month for pure and simple enjoyment, and I read others for business.

Cultural hobbies. I think you should always do something to enhance your appreciation for the innate human ability to be artistically creative. Enjoying the theater, movies, plays, museums, concerts, and dance are all wonderful ways to experience the gift of talent in others. I also suggest that you should bring out the creative side of yourself. Writing short stories, thoughts, poetry; learning to play an instrument; painting, sculpting, dancing, and acting: anything that allows you to express *your* creative side allows you to go outside yourself and to share the fantasy that is creativity.

I "play" the guitar. I've played it off and on for about 25 years. I really enjoy the sound of the instrument; and have always thought that, since I really like music, have rhythm, and can dance, that I should be able to "get down and get funky" on the guitar. Well, after years and years of self-paced playing for my own enjoyment, I still don't get down and funky. For some reason, I just haven't been able to transfer what I perceive to be my funkiness into the guitar. This would be a serious challenge if I played the guitar for a living. My lack of funkiness on the guitar is a source of amusement to me and probably to anyone who has listened to me attack the guitar. Of course, I know how to solve this issue. I could take lessons and the whole bit; but I just like strumming on the guitar as it is; and as funk-impaired as I am, I don't plan to do anything about it but enjoy it.

But the point is this: while I am playing the guitar, the guitar is all there is. Sometimes when there are a lot of things on my mind, I play; and a few minutes later, my thoughts are sorted out, or an idea is crystallized, or a solution presents itself. By focusing your conscious mind, your subconscious takes over and addresses the issue or challenge that may be brewing. In the end, hobbies are not only enjoyable and fun; they are therapeutic.

THE FIVE PHYSICAL SECRETS

Remember, it takes energy to live a successful life. Remember the basics:

1. Diet, water, rest and exercise
2. Physical, mental, and cultural hobbies
3. Self-preservation
4. Prevention
5. Enjoy yourself

The Emotional Key

"I feel good."-James Brown

Today was a good day. Yesterday was a good day. Odds are tomorrow will be a good day. I can't predict or control what will happen tomorrow, but I do have a large degree of control over *how I will react* to what happens tomorrow. Based on how I live my life, I average about 360-plus good days per year. So, most likely, tomorrow will be a good day. This prediction or anticipation is more akin to a self-fulfilling prophecy than manifest destiny. I believe that, by discovering your identity, establishing a spiritual life perspective, maintaining a healthy body, developing emotional balance, and doing things to help others, you develop an outlook that perpetuates optimism on a daily basis. When you awaken and expect things to go and feel well, and reinforce that feeling throughout the day through your attitude and actions, you end up *being* well more often than not.

Your emotional self is a critical part of *Full Life Balance*. You must develop healthy habits and attitudes which allow you to develop and maintain your ability to honestly communicate your emotions, show empathy and compassion, and strive to be a more complete person. As a man, I find this key to be the most difficult one. This is not to say that I have mastered the other keys or found them to be simple undertakings; they are far from that. It is to say that as males, we do show emotion; but many of us have been socially conditioned not to show our full *range* of emotion.

Many men have been encouraged socially to display traditional masculine "leadership" emotions of a calm demeanor; aggressiveness towards an adversary; and

---

the facade of focused, relentless pursuit of a goal. Many of us were not encouraged to develop the traditional feminine "followship and fellowship" emotions of empathy, compassion, and communication of emotion.

Many women generally played games that reinforced the importance of others and the need to nurture and communicate. They played with baby dolls, played house and other games that focused on caring, nurturing, and communicating with and taking care of another person. Girls often apply their compassionate orientation to whatever game they are playing, even if it is a so-called traditionally male sport.

I've watched my sons and daughters play basketball on their respective under-twelve-year-old teams. On the boys' team, if a boy falls and hurts himself, play will normally continue until the point is scored, the ball changes hands, or time-out is called. Then they will go to check on the injured player. Normally, the only boys who show concern, unless it is a serious injury, will be those on the wounded player's team.

In girls' basketball, however, girls from *both* teams will often stop playing to go check on the injured player. These examples are from under-twelve-year-old teams. I have also found that as they get older and more competitive, the reaction of both sexes is nearly identical.

We boys played games that established and reinforced our masculine emotions: games of war, cops and robbers, racing games and others based on the concept "If I win, you lose; if you win, then I lose." Most of these masculine games reinforced the idea that success lies in *overcoming*, not *collaborating or communicating with* or *understanding others*. If we hurt ourselves during the games and went to a parent or

---

older sibling for normal therapeutic psychological comfort, we were often told, "Big boys don't cry," or, "Stop crying like a baby." To avoid this type of ridicule, we learned to repress our true feelings in order to appear tough and strong.

As a result of this unhealthy conditioning, I would suspect that the emotional step of *Full Life Balance* is the most difficult for most males; *and also for, I am sure, a fair number women who have been taught to suppress their emotions, thoughts, and true feelings.* People who were conditioned in this way are simply not accustomed to showing the *range of emotion* they feel; but this only means that they will have to be more vigilant in maintaining emotional balance than others who were conditioned in a healthier manner.

Again, I must mention for the record that I am not an expert by training or by practice in the field of emotional development. I am keenly aware of and often reminded by my own actions and shortcomings that I still have a lot of emotional development ahead; but I want to spend the next few pages sharing my thoughts on this crucial topic, and I hope that you find something useful as you continue on your journey.

A man by himself is more than alone. If you were born and raised to the point of being able to care for yourself, and then left alone on a desert island with all the food, water, and shelter you needed to survive, most experts in human development agree that by the time you became an adult, you would probably be nuttier than a fruitcake. Why? We are gregarious creatures. In order for us to survive and thrive, we need contact with other humans: we need to live in groups in order to live fully. We also need emotional interaction in order to flourish developmentally. (Think back to the elephants.)

51

In order to maintain emotional health, we need to interact with each other on a regular and multi-faceted basis. We need to experience and express joy, sorrow, forgiveness, anger, compassion, ambivalence, and a myriad of other emotions. By experiencing a range of feelings with other people, we in turn become more aware of what it means to be human. I believe that the goal is to understand, appreciate, and enjoy your "up" emotions (like joy, contentment, and excitement) while understanding, appreciating and knowing that it is normal to experience your "down" emotions (such as sadness, anger, and frustration); and realize that neither tends to last forever. Feeling sad occasionally helps you appreciate how precious your up emotions are. I feel up and good almost all the time; but I have and will again experience sadness, tragedy and misfortune. But doesn't it feel good when the emotional rain stops? It is part of being alive and human.

So how do you become emotionally balanced? First, I must remind you that achieving *Full Life Balance* is a process, a process with no defined, specific end point; therefore, the objective is not necessarily to say one day, "I am *perfectly* balanced," although that *would* be wonderful and probably impossible. The objective is to become better than you were before, and strive to be tomorrow and each day after that.

It's like the story of the two businessmen who went on photo safari to the Serengeti in Africa. After arriving and making it to the outskirts of the great range, they spent the night in their guide's tent. The guide told them everything he thought they needed to know in order to have a rewarding and fruitful time photographing some of the world's most precious wildlife. The next day, they were off.

They had a fulfilling early morning, photographing animals of all types. In fact, they became so engrossed in their pictures that they forgot the guide's most stringent warning: "One head up, one head down. One head always looking around." Both men had their heads down, focused on reloading their cameras, when they heard a rustle, then a growling roar in the thigh-high grass fifteen to twenty feet in front of them. As one of the amateur photographers set his camera down and began to tighten the laces on his trail boots, a huge lion sprang from the grass into the clearing just ten feet in front of them. His camera partner said, "Man, don't you know that you can't outrun a lion?" He replied, "I don't have to outrun the lion. I just have to outrun you."

Developing the emotional key to *Full Life Balance* is something like that. We don't need to take on that huge lion of our emotional existence all at once. We just have to outrun or become better at being balanced than we were before; and through this continual striving process, our lives become incrementally better.

The process whereby we can develop our emotional selves is clearly debatable, and I now weigh in with my two cents. I suggest that to be better than we were, we have to **Assess** ourselves, **Cleanse** our undesirable patterns, begin to **Model** emotional balance, **Forgive** ourselves and others when we or they fall short, and **Monitor** our ongoing behavior.

We live in turbulent times. That doesn't mean that we necessarily have to be turbulent people. For many of us, after we realize that there is a powerful and good source, we also realize that we have developed many bad habits and actions (which often are the precursor to the destruction and despair that may lead to a spiritual epiphany). Once these habits are honestly and spiritually assessed, we can begin the processes of

—

cleansing, modeling, forgiving, and monitoring.

Assessing: Do I act like a good or bad person?
While the details of your personal life experience may, on the surface, be readily familiar to you (e.g., you may remember when your parents divorced, or when someone pivotal to your early balance passed away), the long-term social and psychological effects of these experiences aren't as easy to identify and, more importantly, do something about. Many suggest that these early life experiences wield the primary power over most of your adult behavior. It is as if your early life experiences are the software that controls you. You might reach a point where you want to do good, be good, and show others by your actions the power of goodness. However, it might not be clear to you what *is* good. There might be times when you are doing bad and calling it good; or, as constantly demonstrated on the news and "court" television shows, doing bad and justifying the bad behavior.

I've found that one of the best ways to assess yourself is to analyze your behavior in different situations. However, since at times it is somewhat difficult to evaluate yourself while you are in the middle of a situation or circumstance, you will find meditation to be a very useful behavioral assessment tool. When you take quiet time to look at and reflect on how you act and react to life's various situations, you will see patterns emerge; and you will see yourself, like it or not, for what you really are.

There are various ways of assessing yourself: you can call on *the spirit* through prayer; visit professionals in the field of human behavior; take courses, seminars and workshops designed to bring enlightened self-assessment; and more. As always, I recommend the method that works best for you. However, I believe the most essential key to self-assessment, regardless of method, is honesty. In order to truly see yourself, you must honestly address what you see. It is important to assess your behavior, and equally important to assess the thought process that led to the behavior. What you *think* leads to what you do; but what you *do* becomes you in the eyes of the world. The world learns what you really think by your actions.

In addition to analysis by reflection, you must also look at yourself from the perspective of others to see how your actions are perceived. You should ask for their opinions. Questions such as, "What did you think when I said what I said?" and "How does what I did make you feel?" are invaluable when trying to ascertain how others perceive you.

The process of self-assessment is an ongoing one. As dynamic beings who live in dynamic and ever-changing environments, you are subject to many forces and challenges that will influence your behavior. Therefore, true self-assessment is also self-observation. You must observe the conditions and circumstances that lead to certain behavior. This will allow you to develop a better picture of what triggers your various behaviors. Then you are better suited to address them in the **Cleansing** phase.

Cleansing: Getting rid of the bad. In the Baptist church, this is attempted via prayer and confession of sins; in Dianetics, it's attempted via Clearing, a process that employs recalling, analyzing, and diluting the power and effect of negative early memories. In Alcohol Anonymous (AA), it's through completing the fourth of the twelve steps to sobriety, the written itemization and sharing of "character defects" with a sponsor; in Catholicism it is attempted via the personal confession of sins to a priest; and in Buddhism, it is via the

———

meditation technique known as Vipassana. These are just examples. There are, of course, many other methods espoused by many other individuals and entities.

Professionals in the study of the mind, religious organizations, and self-development advocates all point to the fact that we need to somehow address our programmed negative behavior. There are various ways to work on this. The emphasis here is to *work* on yourself. Don't merely accept your negative behavior and justify it with statements such as, "That's just the way I am." The job is on-going, incomplete, hard to gauge, and varying.

A personal experience with a cleansing technique. I found out about a ten-day meditation and cleansing technique called Vipassana from a co-worker. Vipassana means "to see things as they really are." According to the California Vipassana Centers' brochure, it is "a logical process of mental purification through self-observation…" where you "…experience peace and harmony... (because)… it purifies the mind, freeing it from suffering and the deep-seated causes of suffering." It is one of India's most ancient meditation techniques and was practiced by Gotama the Buddha some 2,500 years ago. The underlying concept of this technique is that there is sensation in every part of you. Millions upon millions of cells are being created and destroyed at an almost unimaginable rate throughout the body. This cellular life and death contributes to the sensations you can feel (you know, how sometimes there is a weird itch or slight pain or strange sensation in a part of your body; then as quickly as it comes, it's gone.) when you hone your attention and focus it on a specific area. The goal is to allow you to get in touch with all the sensations of your body and to try to uncover sections that aren't alive with sensitivity. Once these reduced sensation areas are identified, you consciously observe and focus on that part in order to assess and understand the reason for the reduced sensation; then work to cleanse it.

Participants are cautioned not to relish or crave the pleasant sensations they might encounter, and not to dread the undesirable feelings. This is a key point in the Vipassana practice. Practitioners claim that the root of most of our misery lies in our attraction to and repulsion from various external stimuli. We crave the car, the house, the money, the beautiful partner. When our wants aren't met, we feel anxious, envious and miserable. Conversely, we naturally want to retreat from all unpleasant sensations in an unrealistic attempt to live life without the eventualities of life, the ebb and flow and ups and downs of life.

Practitioners claim that the deeper you go into the meditation, the more you discover that the lack of sensation, vague sensations, even pain, may have been associated with some prior emotional event or trauma. Then, by repeatedly scanning this event and the related sensations, you can reduce the effect the event or trauma has on your current behavior. You try to develop equanimity towards the good and bad feelings in order to reduce the influence of emotional craving and aversion in your life. Vipassana also attempts to help you realize that all of your feelings start from within; it's not about what happens to you. It is about how you *react or feel* about what happens. The ideal end result would be the elimination of negative behavior and reactions that purely exist as a result of prior negative experiences. This elimination should, in theory, lead to a more mature emotional outlook and therefore a more enjoyable life.

So, being game to experience all of the above, I decided to check it out. The retreat I attended is located just outside of the little town of North Folk in rural central California.

There are three basic stages to learning the practice of Vipassana: Agreement, Anapana and Vipassana.

Stage 1) Agreement: agree to refrain from killing any living thing; speaking; stealing; using any intoxicants; and all sexual activity for *ten days* while attending the ten-day Vipassana retreat. Over the first three days, I was taught –

Stage 2): Anapana: how to develop a more stable and concentrated mind by learning to fix my conscious attention on the natural reality of the ever-changing flow of the breath as it enters and leaves my nostrils. This "concentration of consciousness" meditation technique is the prelude to attempting the third and final stage. By focusing your conscious mind on the simple task of breathing, you allow your subconscious mind to surface and to be used for reflection, self-inspection and more.

At this point, you are probably wondering how focusing on the natural, consistent and relentless flow of my breath could help me cleanse myself of "deep-seated causes of suffering." So was I; but I wanted to give it a fair shot, so I committed myself to follow all the instructions to the letter.

By the fourth day, as a result of simply focusing my entire conscious mind on my respiration, I had developed the ability to pinpoint my concentration on any and every part of my body. This ability proved important, because I would spend the next six days practicing –

———

58

Stage 3) Vipassana (to see things as they really are): guiding my consciousness to examine and appreciate the physical sensation throughout my entire being.

I was instructed to concentrate my full attention on the soft section at the top of my head. Once I could feel whatever sensation was there, I was to do likewise with the rest of my body. I scanned every part, literally from head to toe, spending fifteen seconds to a minute focused on each area, staying put just long enough to notice the sensation. I could feel movement, blood pumping, heat and the like in most sections. I also noticed something curious: some parts were almost numb. I couldn't pick up any sensation. We were instructed to spend time focusing on the sections that were devoid of feeling. As I did this, various experiences from childhood to adulthood flooded into my consciousness. I saw myself reliving situations that apparently still carried some emotional weight with me. I saw people I still harbored resentment or similar emotions against, whom I thought I had forgiven. I was aware of how my respiration would accelerate as I replayed certain emotion-packed situations and thoughts.

While scanning my body and memories, I realized that I still resented my biological father because of his treatment of me after he and my mom divorced. As I mentioned, as a kid, I had wanted to be around my dad. I thought he was everything, and I looked up to him. Even with his mistreatment of my mom, I still thought he was great. My parents divorced when I was about nine years old, and I missed him deeply.

While meditating, I got in touch with memories of my tenth birthday, and how I felt when he didn't call. I had cried from hurt and anger. As I went deeper, I recalled how, by the time I was thirteen, I didn't care if he called or not. At age fourteen, I promised myself that if I ever had children, regardless of what happened to their mother and me, they would always know that they had a father who loved them.

Getting in touch with these memories caused me to decide that I need to completely forgive him. As I repeatedly scanned through my body, focusing on the areas that were initially numb to my consciousness, it seemed as if the negative effect of these feelings began to diminish. Gradually, apparently corresponding to the diminishing negative feelings, I began to gain sensation in the parts of my body that were previously numb to my consciousness. What remained mostly was the feeling that I needed to do whatever was necessary to clean things up, to clear things up.

During Vipassana, I had my second and possibly most important epiphany. I wanted to understand more about God. I wanted to understand more about religion and spirituality. While mediating, I kept posing various questions to my spirit, such as, "What is life? What does God want? What is spirituality? What is religion in relation to God? Is there only one true religion?" The answers that came up for me were so clear, so real, and so spiritually logical to me that I came away from the retreat without any doubt as to what God wants.

I believe that God the spirit wants us to cut out the man-made religious clutter, to seek the spirit and love each other. Essentially, God the spirit wants us to do good, be good, and show others by our actions the power of goodness. My beliefs are well-documented in the spiritual section.

As I reflect on my experience with Vipassana, it was unbelievable. The intensity of the thoughts and emotions I was able to get in touch with shocked me. I now use some of the meditation techniques in my life daily. My personal jury is still out in regards to the claim of "… mental purification through self-observation;" but, there is definitely something to this type of intense introspection, and I can see the potential value of consistent practice.

Incidentally, upon my return, I did apologize to several folks. I also honestly forgave others, thereby releasing some of the negative feelings I had harbored deep inside towards them. That does not mean that I have wonderful flowing relationships with all those whom I have forgiven or those who I have asked to forgive me. What it means is simply this: I no longer carry around the negative weight I once carried, and I have reduced the power and effect of those incidents over my thoughts and actions. And that, my friends, is a huge starting point.

Overall, I was impressed with the process. I believe it has merit and deserves further investigation and practice; and, as a method for obtaining deeper insight to one's self, I found it to be fascinating. I highly recommend that you look into it.

The cleansing step is obviously a difficult one. Keep in mind that it took years for you to become what you are; therefore, it will take some time and considerable effort to modify and cleanse what you are. But you must attempt to look at yourself and understand your actions at a deeper level; and continue to look for safe, effective methods to accomplish this. Once you cleanse some of your negative emotional garbage through whichever method you choose, you will feel as if you have a clean slate, a new emotional palate on which to paint the next series of pictures in your life. You will no longer be *as burdened* by the weight of past mistakes. You are then ready for the **Modeling** phase.

Modeling: Imitating the desired behavior. Once you are clear — that is relatively clean of spirit, mind, and body pollutants — you can truly discern the actions and activities of those who are acting and being in the emotional light. They spend time with their children, they interact with their significant others, and they communicate their personal truth to those around them. They are actively trying to be emotionally balanced people. Seek them out. They will recognize you and help you develop.

Some of these people you currently know; some you don't. You must observe and then demonstrate the behavior you want to develop. That's the essence of modeling. (Maybe this step should be called "assimilating," because the goal here is to learn, observe, incorporate, assimilate, and adapt the desired behavior. I settled on the term "modeling" because once you find those living in FLB, FLB suggests that you become a model of those traits and attributes for the world.)

FLB is about being true to you and releasing the spirit that lies within all of us. But sometimes you need help in various aspects of your life. You should seek people who demonstrate the emotional characteristics that you are trying to develop. Then do what they do. Read what they read. Learn how they think and try to understand why.

Forgiving: Accepting our humanity. We are not perfect, but that realization should not hinder us from seeking perfection. *Seeking* perfection is totally different from *expecting* or *requiring* perfection of ourselves and others. Therein lies the need for you to expand your capacity to forgive. You will make mistakes, hurt others' feelings, ignore the obvious, and generally do the wrong thing emotionally again and again in your life; but by working on your emotional self from a positive point of view (you can be at least a little better than you were before), you will reduce the incidences of emotional insensitivity in your life and, as a result, become a more emotionally balanced person.

My best friend, Rev. Robert (Bobby, to me) Duncan and I (Billy, to him) get together once a month or so to discuss what we consider the important things in life. This discussion has become a tradition for us. We've been doing it for nearly thirty years. We discuss the diverse aspects of our lives: our youth in Hunters Point; college times; the birth and growth of our children; the various changes, twists and turns of our careers; and our general development as men. I have been able to honestly share the good, bad, ups, and downs with Bobby. We have disagreed, argued, shouted, laughed, and prayed with each other. We have, through these discussions, seen each other through divorces, deaths, and revelations. Bobby is a true friend to me and I to him. I love him and I know he loves me. (For emotional health, you need to have a honest, safe place(s) where you can express everything you feel. For those of you who do not have such a network in place, I strongly suggest you cultivate one. And please pay close attention to the following discussion on the effect of not being able to adequately respond to external factors emotionally.)

Bobby and I have always envisioned ourselves as philosophers, and would rarely shy away from a discussion on any aspect of life and its wide-ranging realities and possibilities.

During one of our discussions, we talked about why so many people have such seemingly short emotional fuses. How some get so upset so often and so quickly, then commit actions that create the need for an apology and/or plea for forgiveness. We concluded that many people *simmer* emotionally and therefore are easy to bring to a *boil.* Envision your emotions as water in a pot on a stove, with a lukewarm temperature being the normal, calm emotional state. Simmering then is the emotional state of constant, low-level agitation; and the state of being upset is boiling.

We talked further about how this propensity affects all ages and backgrounds. We began to find commonalities in this broad group, including but not limited to: *the inability to express emotion and thought; the perception (or reality) of receiving disparate treatment; unfufilled dreams and expectations; and a general feeling of not being in control of their lives.*

Often when a person with this combination of thoughts and feelings encounters a circumstance where they feel that they are being taken advantage of, such as becoming unemployed, being denied some type of benefit, divorce, even being cut-off in traffic — in short, when they feel disrespected or mistreated in any way — this person may act out, often violently, in an attempt to demonstrate that they, not others, are in control of their own lives. Some of the syptoms of the simmering and boiling syndrome may be road rage, wife abuse when the husband's football team loses, and full family-on-family fights at Chuck E. Cheese®; all of which seem to be appearing more frequently in the news.

Of course, there are many variations on this theme; and this is by no means an attempt to justify any violence, mental, emotional or physical abuse inflicted on anyone by someone who could not understand,

———

64

process and release their anger, frustration and resentment in a healthy way. This is simply an attempt to paint a part of the picture as it exists. Many men, women and children who have difficulty processing and releasing frustration and anger may be constantly simmering poised to boil.

But again, these realizations are not a justification to continue to boil. At some point, you must develop the ability to process your anger and frustration, and cease to constantly simmer in apparent preparation for boiling. Someone once said something like it's not your fault for being knocked down, but it is your fault for not trying to get up.

By identifying the big picture, you can use it as background for the emotional development and anger management work you have ahead if you are to experience the joy and fulfilment of *Full Life Balance*. Strive to turn anger, resentment, and bitterness into healthy, positive action. Simmering and boiling are reactions to what happens to you. For the most part, *how you react to a situation is more important than the situation.* You must learn how to avoid taking your societal frustrations out on your family, friends, other loved ones, and your community in general. Our prisons are full of men and women who could not successfully process their anger and frustration.

Tips on Forgiveness. No matter how balanced you are, you will need to ask for forgiveness. You are human. You will make mistakes and hurt someone's feelings. Three things are crucial when asking for forgiveness: honesty, specificity, and timeliness.

- *Be honest.* When asking for forgiveness, you should honestly want to be forgiven. You should not ask for forgiveness because that's what you think the other person wants you to

65

do. You should ask for forgiveness when you honestly believe you have done something, inadvertently or deliberately, that has harmed another.

- *Be specific.* You should clearly specify what you did, why you are sorry, and that you want forgiveness for it. Simply saying, "I'm sorry" is not enough because it is too generic and leaves the door open for misunderstanding and recurrence of the situation. If you clearly state the issue, why you were wrong, and that you want forgiveness for the act, you will make it clear that you know what you did to offend; and that you do not intend to repeat the offense.

- *Be timely.* You should apologize within a reasonable time frame. During the middle of the argument may not be the best time; but please don't let days and weeks go by before you attempt to mend an emotional fabric you have torn. Over time, feelings crystallize and permanent changes and attitudes develop. Would you want a person you care about to develop a permanent negative feeling towards you because of a mistake, when you could possibly clear it up with an apology? Probably not; so act in a timely manner.

Monitoring: Check yourself. You must monitor your actions and behaviors. I am not suggesting constant second-guessing or paranoia, but you should look at what you do, what you say, how you act, and how others perceive all of the above on an ongoing basis.

You are a fascinatingly complex and dynamic being who exists in a fascinatingly complex and dynamic environment. Neither you nor your environment will ever be exactly the same as yesterday. Therefore, it is vital that you monitor your thoughts and actions constantly.

You should celebrate and reward yourself for what you are and the good that you do. By the same token, you should forgive yourself and make realistic and conscious efforts not to repeat the instances where your actions were less than your capabilities. I conclude this chapter by discussing how you can use this key to open the door to rich, rewarding relationships.

Relationships: Partner, Children, Families and Friends. In addition to yourself, the beneficiaries of your focus, analysis, and adjustment of emotional behavior will be those who are closest to you — your partner, children, family, and friends. The personal result of this analysis and adjustment can be your increased feelings of well-being, value, and usefulness.

I have found the following words and phrases (and more importantly, the sincere thoughts and actions connected to them) to be some of the most important that you can use in relationships with those closest to you:

"I'm sorry, I was wrong when I ...."

"What do you think?"

"Excuse me."

"When you do...., it makes me feel ......"

"I like what you did because...."

"Let me turn this off/put this away — so I can listen to you." And,

---

67

"Were you watching that channel?"☺

Of course, there are many more ways to say you care and respect someone. Try to find them and earnestly use them often.

What do you think? Will people always tell you what they think? No. Many times, action or lack of action gives you a clue as to what is going on in the mind of another, but not always accurately. Also, for different reasons, those near and dear to you may not always feel comfortable just volunteering their thoughts.

For example, when children are very young, they tend to want to tell their parents everything. However, as they get older, they generally keep more of their thoughts and feelings to themselves.

So how do you find out what they think? One of the best ways is to just ask them, "What do you think?" If you begin asking your child about their thoughts in toddler hood, chances of your having an open and comfortable relationship for this dialog in later years are greater. If the first time you ask your daughter what she thinks is when she is fourteen, the odds of receiving any valuable feedback are slim, and the discussion will probably be awkward. If you ask early and often, you greatly increase the chance of receiving good feedback, even when she goes through the all-parents-are-stupid phase.

Listen. Your partner, children, siblings, parents, other family, and friends are just like you. They want respect, love, attention, and to feel good. When you ask, "What do you think?" of your three-year old toddler or your ninety-three-year old grandmother, you only need to do one thing for them to feel you truly value their opinion: **listen**. Be quiet on both the outside and on the inside: no extra movement; eyes focused on them; think about the words they are saying and the feelings behind those words, not what you are going to say in response. You should endeavor to create an environment around you that allows and encourages others to share with you. This applies not only to exchanges with your children, but with all of your relationships — especially with your life partner, other family, and friends.

A few years ago, my then-twelve-year old son William II called me one evening.

"Hi, Dad."

"What's up Wink?"

"Nothing."

So I asked, "How was school today?"

"Oh, ok."

Now, just to clearly paint the picture. He called me. Maybe he was just saying hi; but maybe he wanted to say something, but he's not telling yet. That tells me that what he wants to tell me is either something bad or something personal. So I know it's going to require some digging on my part. And some attentive, active, below-the-surface listening. After some more small talk, I went back to the school line of questioning.

"So, what happened today at school that made you laugh?"

"Nothing, really."

"Nothing?"

"Well..., this girl kissed me." Aha! That was the reason for the call. A girl had kissed him, and now he had finally told me.

"A girl kissed you? Tell me about it. What happened?"

I then proceeded to learn about the girl, the circumstances surrounding the kiss, if this was the first kiss, and the prospects for further such contact with said girl or others.

The lesson in this instance was to be patient; to listen not only to what was being said, but *how* it was being said; and to continue to ask questions. William II wanted to tell me; I just had to make it easy for him to do so.

When my daughter Eunique was about five-years old, I described parts of the body to her using a car analogy. I likened the heart to an engine, the grill to the nose, the carburetor for the lungs, and so on. About a year or two after that enlightening conversation, she came up to me, looking strange, and said, "My motor is running fast."

I said, "What?"

I felt her chest and realized that her heart was beating nearly twice the normal rate. We rushed her to the hospital and discovered that she had infrequent cardiac arrhythmia. I relate this illustration for two reasons: 1) I listened to her at a very important time, and 2) she not only listened to me but remembered what I had said. If you listen to your children, they will listen, for the most part, to you. For maximum effect, begin listening at birth and do it forever.

Tell your children. Tell them that you love them. Tell them what you like about them. Tell them that you are glad that they are your children. Tell them about the

—

70

good parts of you that you see in them. Tell them about your childhood. Tell them the truth: the partial truth when they are young and whole truth when they are mature enough. Were you a good kid? A bad kid? Did you fight? Did you earn good grades? Bad grades? Tell them about your parents. Tell them about what you did to receive a punishment. Tell them about the punishments. Tell them about your brothers and sisters. Tell them that you pray for them. If you don't pray, tell them that you think about them. Tell them that you thank the spirit for them. Tell them about smoking, drugs, alcohol, and AIDS. When you tell them about you, in reality you are telling them about them.

Share with your children. Share your thoughts, dreams, and fears with your children. Share your past with them. Share a secret with them. Share with them what makes you happy, sad, embarrassed, or lonely. Share a financial gain with them and tell them why they've earned it. Share good and bad stories with them. Share your opinion on political, social, and current events. Share household chores with them. Just share with them.

Ask your children. Ask your children to help you accomplish something. Ask them to teach you something. Ask them to show you something. Ask them what makes them feel happy, sad, nervous, or embarrassed. Ask them what their favorite song, movie, video game, rapper, team, car, clothes, food, vacation spot, or book is. You get the idea — ask them about their interests. Ask them if they have been offered or use drugs, cigarettes or alcohol. Ask them if they have a girlfriend, boyfriend, study friend. Ask them what they like about that person.

———

My then seventeen-year-old son, Robert (Robster!☺) and I had a talk about talent (actually, the talk began on the subject of his most recent grades and evolved into a discussion about talent). Quite sometime prior to this talk, I had asked him about movies he liked. In addition to *The Man Without a Face* with Mel Gibson, one of his favorite movies was Robert DeNiro's *A Bronx Tale*.

The film is about a father (DeNiro) who tries to hold on to his relationship with and influence over his only son, who is being swayed from the straight and narrow by an up-and-coming mafia boss. DeNiro's character is a hard-working bus driver who is trying to do the best for his family. Several times he tells his son that it is important for him to use his talents. He says, "The worst thing in the world is wasted talent. It's an insult to God."

Robert has been blessed with loads of talent. He is an intelligent, atheltic, personable, and friendly young man. He has what I call the "full package." He has incredible potential and academic talent — that is being underutilized. Knowing that he likes *A Bronx Tale*, I quoted DeNiro's speech from the movie as I tried to make the point that I felt he was not fully using his talent. Did that referrence totally change his life and his academic effort? Of course not (well, not yet, at least). But I showed him that I try to pay attention to and remember what he likes. Robert knows I know what some of his favorite movies are. That's gotta' count for something.

Thank your children. Thank your children for being who they are. Thank them for doing something around the house. Thank them for good grades, a good efforts, good attendance, good attitudes. Thank them for choosing their friends and tell them why you are thanking them for those particular friends. Thank them for listening. Thank them for not being a negative statistic quoted on the six-o'clock news. Just thank them.

(In each of the four sections above, just replace the words "your children" with "your partner," "your family," and "your friends" to get the big picture, if you haven't already.)

Your children should be able to finish sentences such as, "My dad thinks…", "he believes in…", "My mom likes when I…", "She expects me to…." In short, your children should know enough about you to say that *they know you*. You should also be able to complete similar sentences regarding them. *It's your job to make sure that they know you and know what you stand for.* Someone once said, "If you don't stand for something, you will fall for anything." I also like the saying that goes something like, "If our children choose to be fools, it's mostly their failure; but if they didn't have a choice because we never showed them the difference — it's mostly our failure."

Make time. You are busy. You have to be; but you must *make time*. Before I began my MBA studies, I was busy. Adding the requirements of an accelerated MBA program to my schedule was a difficult challenge. I did most of my homework during the evening between nine and one o'clock in the morning. This, of course, was a major blow to my personal time with my sweetie, Linda. Luckily, our offices were close to each other.

We began a ritual of sharing lunch three to four times per week in order to make sure that we spent quality face-time together. This helped us maintain some relationship normalcy during a relatively brief but extremely hectic period of time. You have got to have some time with your partner. Time to talk about the two of you, life, children, bills — you know, the entire deal, without being too absorbed in thoughts of homework or

73

being too tired to be an active participant. We have
continued the practice, and it still works.

THE FIVE EMOTIONAL SECRETS
**The emotional key may require the most work for
most of us.**

1. **Assess your behavior.**
2. **Cleanse negative attitudes.**
3. **Model desirable behaviors.**
4. **Forgive yourself and others — honestly,
    specifically and in a timely fashion.**
5. **Listen, thank, ask, tell, share, and MAKE
    TIME.**

The Professional Key

"You could be the world's best garbage man, the world's best model, it doesn't matter what you do if you're the best."- Muhammad Ali

"Oz never did give nothing to the Tin Man, that he didn't already have."- from the song "The Tin Man," by America

This key addresses the need to not only have gainful employment, but the need to excel at everything you do. I use the term "professional" in the context of doing everything you do *well*. From managing your finances to maintaining your home and car, to career development and academic pursuits: all of these areas of your life require you to be professional if you are to Live Better Everyday® on the road to a fully balanced life.

Gainful employment. You have to work. If you live to seventy years of age, you will spend approximately forty of those years in the work force. At eight hours per day, five days per week, fifty weeks per year, you will spend an average of 3,333 continuous days working. That is the equivalent of working all day, everyday, twenty-four hours per day for over nine consecutive years of your life. The only activity that you participate in more than work is sleep. Of course, for many the numbers are much higher. If you are going to spend so much of your time working, shouldn't you be doing something you are good at and enjoy?

A crucial part of this key is to understand that it is not just *what* you do, *how* you do it, *why* you do it, *how much* you get paid to do it, or *how much* you enjoy it—*it's all of these things; they are all connected.* The vocational stage of the professional key of *Full Life Balance* is

75

designed to help put you in a position to do the thing you really *want* to do and are *gifted* to do for a living — knowing that if you truly want to do it, you will become very good at it; and that the rest (good income, job satisfaction) will follow. That is vocational success.

While pursuing my MBA, I took an economics course from a fascinating man, the late Professor Joe Furhrig. Joe introduced us to the widely held concept of "relative or proportional wants." He said that most of humankind's economic and social behavior could be explained by understanding that we are driven by wants. The premise is simple: *the reason we do what we do is because we want to; and we will continue doing that particular thing until our desire to do something else becomes greater than our desire to continue doing what we are doing*. It's similar to the scientific principles an object in motion tends to stay in motion, and an object at rest tends to stay at rest.

To illustrate, let's take George. He is a hypothetical toll-taker on the San Francisco Bay Bridge (George could also be a stockbroker, a plumber, a doctor — any occupation). According to Joe, the reason George is still a toll-taker on the bridge, even as he sees the new automated fast-track lanes springing up to the left and to the right of him, is because he doesn't *want* to learn to do something else *more* than he wants to stay as he is; and, as a result, he will watch himself be automated out of a job.

George knows the proverbial house is on fire and that he should get out, but his desire is not strong enough to cause him to make the move — take courses, attend job fairs, see a vocational counselor — to equip himself for the next career.

76

You may say (as we said in class), "But George has to work because he has to eat to live."

Joe would reply, "Yes. George does have to work. But does he have to work *that* job?"

"But, jobs are hard to find."

And Joe might respond, "Not if you have the right skills. In the long run, the person who is prepared will find employment. *You may have to temporarily continue in a position that you don't want while training for the position you do want.*"

To expand on Joe's concept and to paraphrase Maslow's Needs Hierarchy, we address our true "needs" at the subconscious level — the need to breath, eat, drink, sleep, find a love interest, and the like. We address our wants or desires at the conscious level — what job, which food, which partner, where to sleep, etc. The conscious area is the area of choice. All of us will weigh the choices in one form or another, and then act on them.

Back to the example of George. Let's say that back when George decided to take the job as a toll-taker, it was the only position in his world that he was qualified for at the time. Time passes, and George continues to work and continues to watch as the number of automated fast-track lanes increases. He should be able to see that the writing on the wall foretells the end of his current career. If George *desires* going home after work and watching television, going to dinner, hanging out with his friends, or whatever, *more than he desires* continued employment, he will do nothing to substantially change his circumstance. Until he wants to change the status quo, he will not prepare himself for his next career. He will not look for other positions. In the near future, George will wake up and find himself deemed professionally obsolete.

The concept of relative want applies to all aspects of our lives. We will use this as an underlying theme for this section. We must eat, we desire to sleep in a sheltered environment, we need to wear clothing, use transportation, and a myriad of technological devices. The things we use, need, and want cost money. Therefore, just as we kids used to say, "We have got to get paid."

You have to do something well enough for someone to want to pay you. Be it as an employee, contractor, or owner; someone has got to value your services enough to give you money. Since you need to get paid, you have to work, unless you are retired or live off your inheritance and investments. You may retain most of the money that your work and knowledge generates, or relatively little; but you must generate income to meet your needs.

In this section, we will help you look at *your attitude about what you do* (which has a direct connection to how much you get paid); how to *identify your career*; the concept of a *transitional job versus a career position*; how to *master habits*; and other areas of your life that require your professionalism.

Let's start by looking at what you do to earn income. Whether you have had years of training and education for your current position, or you just dropped out of the sky, picked up an application and began to work, you probably are gainfully employed in at least one job or career. You may be one of the substantial number that has two jobs, or you may even go to work and go to school.

For discussion purposes, I want to distinguish between the skilled trades (such as electrician, plumber, carpenter) and general blue-collar work (street sweeper, laborer, bus driver, bridge toll-taker). The latter — the general blue-collar field — is where I want to focus for just a moment. Many positions in this area are undergoing upheaval. Over the last ten years, many positions in this space have become obsolete. You may need to make some immediate decisions if you work in any area, be it white- or blue- collar, where the job is repetitive, labor-intensive, and uses low or little technology. Also, because of the repetitive and manual nature of the work, I suspect that this is an area of low job satisfaction.

If you are in this type of occupation, you must ask yourself, "How long will I be able to do what I currently do for a living?" If you can see obvious signs, as in our example with George and the automated fast-track lanes, you would be best advised to begin planning for your next career.

I have had a few eye-opening, course-correcting experiences with the field of blue-collar labor. While I was in college, I had the opportunity to work as a busboy at Candlestick Park, the current home of the San Francisco 49ers and the former home of the *mighty* San Francisco Giants.

As I poured coffee and water, cleaned tables, and worked as a general *gofer*, I found consolation in reminding myself that I was in college and that I would not work as a busboy for a living. But the most telling incident for me, the encounter that made it crystal-clear that I was *not* cut out to do general blue-collar work, occurred the summer after my Candlestick Park experience.

The realization was facilitated by my dad, the late Mr. Bobbie Campbell (Hey, Pops☺). At the time, he worked as a longshoreman on the San Francisco waterfront. I was a freshman in college when my dad asked if I wanted to make some money. Of course, I said, "Yes." He said that I could make about eight bucks an hour (this was 1973, when the minimum wage was about $2.50), so I was estatic about the chance to get *paid*. The job was during the swing shift, as I recall, around four in the afternoon to twelve midnight. Pops told me that I might get "a little dirty." I would, however, do almost anything, at anytime, for eight bucks an hour. So let's go.

The scheduled day arrived. I'm a bright-eyed, bushy-tailed college student ready to make big money. All I had to do was get my hands "a little dirty." Here's the scene: we walked onto a huge cargo ship in the midst of the waterfront. This was back when every day, *tens of thousands* of men at shipping ports all across this country, with hand carts, dollies, and forklifts unloaded millions and millions of dollars' worth of merchandise that the U.S. imported, exported, and transported, box by box. Compare that to today, when large cargo containers are unloaded by only a *few thousand men* across the country operating huge cranes faster and cheaper. (Hmmm… George, are you listening?) The waterfront was a lively, exciting, robust place, with dive bars, illegal gambling joints, *extremely* colorful women, and greasy-spoon diners. It was a feast for the senses: the noise, provocative smells, the language. It was cool. I felt like I was a real man. Just being with my dad, going to do real manly work with other real manly men — there was something about that experience that sticks with me to this day. It was special.

Back to the story. As we went down into the boiler room of the ship, I noticed two things: no one was working; and it was the dirtiest, greasiest place I had ever been in my life. But hey, at eight dollars an hour, I was thinking about how I was going to use my easy money. There were about twelve men sitting around talking, listening to the radio, playing cards — doing everything but working. They acknowledged my dad and made a point to say, "Hey," to me. He proudly told them that I was his son (My dad never introduced us as his step-children. We were his children.) who was in college studying business. To show my eagerness to work, I boldly asked him what he wanted me to do, in front of the other men. He said that we (meaning me) had to clean the boiler.

I was led to something that looked like two huge, oily pots with connecting pipes protruding from the top and sides of each. They were about ten feet wide and twelve feet high, and looked like beer vats you see at breweries and on Budweiser ™ commercials. This was the boiler. Below it was an open area about two-and-one-half feet high, about ten feet wide, and about ten feet deep.

I remember thinking, *He'll probably want me to wash the outside of this thing.* Just then he said, "All you have to do is slide into that area below the boiler, scoop out the build-up on the bottom, fill the bucket with it, pass it out, and repeat until it's clean enough to spray wash. You'll be done in a few hours."

I remember saying, "*Under* the boiler?"

He said, "Yes," and I went to work. It was the most disgusting thing I had ever experienced. Under the boiler was a build-up of oil, grease, and crap about 2 to 3 inches thick. I was given a small hand shovel and a bucket with a rope on it. After I filled the bucket with the fetid crud, I would shout out; and someone would pull the bucket out, empty it, and return it for another load. So as I lay in the crud, scooping, squinting, and trying not to breathe the stuff, I kept saying to myself, *I will get my degree; I will master my skills; and never, I will never have to do this kind of work again.* I could hear those guys laughing about it and at the look on my face when I saw the scope of the job.

My not-so-promising summer career as a longshoreman, or more specifically as a boiler cleaner, was over. It lasted all of one shift, about eight hours. I couldn't take it. All I remember thinking was, *I am going to school and I'm going to be a businessman.* That was just what Dad wanted and his friends expected. They apparently had seen it all before. I could hear them comparing me to someone else's son who had experienced the same career-affirming process just a few days earlier.

Later, I realized that since my dad and the men he worked with could not teach us (their sons) about the subjects we were studying in college, business, or the stock market, they decided to teach us something about how valuable and important the college experience could be by showing us up close and personal how life would be without it.

My dad passed on over thirteen years ago, and it seems that not a week goes by that I don't thank him in prayer for some lesson or another he taught me. *Thanks, Pops.*

Please don't get me wrong. There is nothing wrong with blue-collar work. It has been the vocational backbone of my family and millions of families like mine; but I stress two points here. 1) Apparently, blue collar work is *wrong for me*. I had to identify what I liked to do, what abilities I was blessed with, *and* what I didn't like to do, in order to *enthusiastically* develop my skills

---

and, as a result, a career in my *gifted area*. 2) Whatever your career choice, be it white, blue, or no collar, please take heed to the lesson of the toll-taker, the longshoreman, and the dinosaur: evolve or die.

Maybe you are reading this book because someone recommended it to you, or you happened to hear or read something about it; but if you are reading it because you attended one of my presentations on *Full Life Balance*, the financial markets, or any other topic, you know what I enjoy doing the most: live audience presentations. It is also what I do best. The bigger the group, the better.

(By the way, my presentation ability was not an accident. Most of my siblings have this ability. You should see and hear my younger brother, Rev. Hugh K. Wesley. I have worked to improve my skills, but I was blessed with early training as a base to build on. When we were little, often before we could go out and play after we had completed our regular homework, our mother made each one us stand in front of the others and read something aloud for a few minutes. My siblings and I probably learned more about Black history during these read-aloud sessions under my mother's instruction than we did at school. While we read, we were instructed to stand straight, look up from the paper, and pronounce our words clearly. At the time, we thought it was some bizarre form of torture because none of our friends had to do it. *Thanks, Mom.*).

If you could see how I am involved with and excited by my audience while giving a presentation, you would see my gifted area.

Let's talk about your attitude about what you do to secure income. I don't know exactly how most people feel about what they do to earn a living, but I would venture a guess, based on comments I've heard over the

---

years. The general feeling is negative for most folks. There is a lot of dissatisfaction in the working world. It seems to me that the Monday, Tuesday, Wednesday…scenario I will outline in the spiritual section may have developed in part because of the feelings most people have towards their occupations. I believe it is extremely difficult to excel at something that you don't enjoy doing or feel good about; and it is difficult to get paid well when you do not excel.

So, how do you excel? Simple: do what you like to do for a living. How do you find what you like to do? Well, how did you find out that you liked donuts? You tried them. Likewise, in order to identify your vocationally gifted area, you have to try things. From researching careers, doing internships, taking courses, and interviewing those who currently work in the desired field, to taking a job or starting your own business in the field: you have to try what's out there. Also, aptitude tests, personality assessments, and similar tools help you to find out what fields best suit your personality.

Once you identify what career best suits you, identify what is needed to achieve it. Accept the fact that it is going to take work to get there. The next step is to visualize (which is absolutely different from fantasizing; more on that later) yourself excelling in the career. Then proceed to develop an attack strategy.

Midway through my MBA coursework, one of my professors, Dr. Michael LoSchavio, dedicated one class session to the practice of finding the correct firm in which to continue our post-MBA career. Dr. LoSchavio suggested a three-pronged attack, which I offer to you (again, assuming you've identified your gifted area):

1) **Find a need and fill it.** Analyze a company's operation, then create a new position that hasn't existed there before (the ideal scenario) or enhance an existing function.
2) **Locate a company that has a philosophy similar to your own.** Two points here: first, try to work in the corporate headquarters. You want to rub shoulders with the head people in the firm. Second, analyze the company style and culture in order to have your moral fabric reinforced rather than challenged, and to avoid being ostracized because of your beliefs, moral standards, and/or character.
3) **Place your package on the highest desk.** Your package includes: an executive summary cover letter; a proposal detailing not only a problem and solution, but also why and how you are an integral part of the solution; and a functional resume targeting the position you are creating. Make sure it lands on the highest level possible in the company. And this person should be expecting it.

Taking his timely advice, I enthusiastically employed Dr. LoSchavio's suggestions.

First, a little background. When I began my degree studies, I was nearing the end of my fourth year as a stockbroker with a large investment firm. I had a long-standing passion and fascination for the financial markets, and I had learned the essence of the retail financial services business. I was also developing my skills as a financial educator and motivator by doing and studying presentations; in short, I was training for my future.

I examined my career, and realized that I enjoyed being a financial educator and motivator more than I did being a broker. My particular passion was to educate people of African descent. I even dreamed of flying from city to city, teaching audience after enthusiastic audience about key aspects of the financial markets, and encouraging them to get involved. Once I made this realization and the decision to move to the next level of my career, being a stockbroker became my transitional job. That's the job you do until you move to the career you want, just as being a toll-taker should be a transitional job for our friend George. (Let's just hope he realizes it in time to make a smooth transition for himself and his family.)

After I analyzed my desires and abilities, my current firm's focus and core competencies, the state and the future of the industry, the strengths and weaknesses of other competitors, and business and social trends, I concluded that my firm would probably invest in the idea of creating a division that would develop and market financial services to a large, growing, under-served and under-invested segment of the country: African Americans. (By the way, this type of analysis can and should be applied to life, job, career, and business in order to discover and then pursue your true vocational path.)

After all, my research had uncovered that people of African descent made over $465 billion in 1998. At the time, that was nearly the equivalent of the gross national product (GNP: the market value of all goods and services produced by the labor and property in a country) of Australia. My research also showed that up until this point, folks of African descent had not developed a strong brand affinity for any particular investment firm, so the door appeared to be wide open for some wise and aware firm to capture this lucrative market.

The research for this proposal became a project for one of my business classes. I solicited help from my MBA cohort, several professors (including an English professor to help critique my documents), and the librarian. Incidentally, while developing my package, I became aware of a company which had a division that was not only already pursuing my target market, but was doing an annual survey of the investment patterns of African Americans.

I completed my research, proposed the creation of a unit headed by me (the title I suggested was Vice-President of Domestic Emerging Markets), developed a package called "Marketing to the African American Church," and solicited and received support for the plan from some of the local and regional officers of the firm.

Now, it was time to attack. I spent the next six months dealing with my firms' New York headquarters, trying to get the concept off the ground. My enthusiasm slowly turned to dismay when it became crystal clear to me that I did not have the requisite support of headquarters to move such a program through the hierarchy. In the end, my attempts at my firm were unsuccessful.

I turned my attention to the firm that was already conducting an African American investor survey and ostensibly had a division that was marketing to them. I thought they would be the next logical choice. I revised my package, began to investigate the company, made some connections, and launched. I found that the company had a philosophy of "education first." It also believed in a no-conflict mode of business — their brokers were not on commission, and the company did not have paid analysts who recommended certain securities and compensated the brokers to sell them.

Therefore, there was not an inherent conflict between the clients' desires, the brokers' motivations, and the firm's business objectives. These practices not only set well with me; but I also felt that these ideas would resonate well with inexperienced investors, specifically, those of African descent who, due to lack of knowledge, lack of trust, and lack of exposure, weren't participating in the financial markets in the same proportion as their European American counterparts.

In addition, this firm's headquarters was in my home town, San Francisco. They didn't have anyone dedicated to the investor education of and relationship development with African Americans. And *that's* what I did best.

On paper it was the perfect scenario and perfect opportunity. So, I tackled them. I was able to get my package on the desk of the Vice-President of their African American Marketing Initiative. After she reviewed it, we had an initial telephone interview. Then she attended what would be my last presentation for my existing firm. It happened to be a presentation to Grambling University's West Coast alumni conference of a seminar I had created called "Who's Driving The Market?"

I gave an overview of the financial markets; statistics on the economic power and investing patterns of African American people; a discussion of economic trends; and suggestions as to what individual investors could do to take advantage of these trends. But what made the presentation special was the fact that I incorporated the old African tradition of call and response, coupled with an appropriate dose of humor and entertaining stories, all designed to make the learning process more enjoyable.

This was the perfect job interview. I was in my element. I had trained for this moment. I stepped up to the plate, focused all my abilities, and swung for the fences. I had practiced and studied my subject matter. I had developed my presentation skills from the basics of posture and voice projection to the more advanced aspects of facilitation, guided audience interaction, and pregnant pauses. In fact, I knew my subject matter so well, that my major focus throughout the seminar was the audience, not the topic. The primary question on my mind was, "Are they getting it?"

There were moments when I felt as if I were outside of my body, watching myself doing the presentation. Fewer than two months later, I began my career as the first Regional Investor Education Specialist for my new firm's nascent African American Marketing Initiative. This position literally had not existed prior to my seeking a career there. They were thinking about bringing a person on board to handle their west coast investor education effort. I happened to make the right approach with the right idea to the right person at the right time.

When I shared the good news with them, my cohort, professors, and librarian celebrated my good fortune, and jokingly called me the poster child for how to create and land the perfect job *while* you're getting your MBA.

This is simply an example of how one can make one's own reality. There are millions of other stories about folks who have done much, much more, and far more successfully than I. Many have overcome far more daunting odds — started successful businesses or began more fulfilling careers or created custom-tailored positions — and are able to have incredible lives, raise wonderful families, and have enough left over to endow needy charities. It's being done every day.

"The smarter and harder I work, the luckier I get." You weren't born with the ability to read. You were born with the ability to *learn* how to read. But that wasn't enough — you had to work hard to be *able* to read. As I observe and assess the people I have come into contact with in my life, I have come to the conclusion that a *major contributor to lasting professional success is not only hard and intelligent work; it is also applying the resulting knowledge to every aspect of our lives.*

Out of 100 people, I think there might be about five who, for whatever reason — genetics, physiology, biology, or other quantifiable physical or mental condition — can't work hard and become intelligent. And I'd guess that there are about the same number who are exceptionally brilliant. Incredibly, hysterically brilliant people. That leaves about 90% who are like the rest of us. We are just good old normal people of average intelligence and ability. Of the folks like you and me, the successful ones at some point in their lives simply committed themselves to working harder and becoming smarter and better at what they do. That is the essential difference between those who achieve lasting professional success and those who don't.

Some people will never succeed; some people will.

Just look at their habits to tell them apart. Oh, some folks may hit the lottery, others may stumble across a hit song; but most of the folks who achieve long-term success are the ones who make an ongoing, long-term commitment to work harder and smarter to be better at what they do, and apply the knowledge and skill they gain to their profession. Would you willingly go to a plumber who didn't know (translation: did not work hard and smart to become better) about plumbing? Or to a doctor who had not completed medical school? Of course not.

The guy who hit the lottery, in order to successfully keep his winnings, must work to quickly learn about money management, develop increased people skills, master his spendthrift desires, and so on. The gal who stumbled upon a hit song must work extremely hard in an attempt to cut a hit album. By the way, show me the star, no matter how hard they work, who can consistently *guarantee* a hit album or a hit movie. It's like trying to find a family that never encountered the life event known as death — impossible. Local bars are full of high school stars who were talented, but never seriously practiced or studied; and now are broken spirits who spend large parts of their time reminiscing and romancing their past glory. "Man, those were the days," and "I coulda gone pro" or some similar lament resonates daily throughout bars across the country. I am not ridiculing failure or unrealized dreams. (Incidentally, *these* are the days. Those days are gone and are fun to remember occasionally, but we are alive now. Today is infinitely more important and valuable than yesterday.) I am just commenting on what it takes to make it. Just ask Bill Gates, Oprah Winfrey, Stevie Wonder, or Yo-Yo Ma.

Connections, timing, physical appearance, race, sex,

and other factors often influence the outcome of any pursuit; however, no one would dispute the fact that these folks and hundreds of thousands of other successful people have talent and are smart in their respective gifted areas. But what turned each of them into legends was essentially an ongoing, long-term commitment to smart and hard work, and the tenacity to strive relentlessly towards a chosen goal. The harder and smarter they worked, the luckier they were.

One last comment on the vocational area: share what you learn about your business with your children. I am a decent manager, but one of the best managers I know is my daughter Rachael. In her early twenties, she worked as a waitress at a casual dining restaurant. She has an incredible way with people and a great process memory. As a result, she constantly received huge tips and commendations.

I suggested that she go into an industry where she could make more money per transaction using her skills. She went into sales, liked it, and nailed it. From there we discussed going into management to show other sales people how to succeed. Again, she killed it. From there we talked about her managing groups of stores; and yes, when she became a district manager, she blew the cover off the ball. I helped her with sales, management, and some perfunctory career path type of things; but she has taken everything I have given her and amplified it.

In addition, she is outstanding in something I've always been poor-to-average in: managing her manager. She knows how to manage up the food chain as well as manage down the line. Rachael currently is a director with a major Fortune 500 company. She is responsible for hundreds of employees, and is widely respected above and below her position. At her pace and with her ability, I would not be surprised if she makes it to the corner office of the C-suite in a major firm sometime in the near future. She is a better manager than I am, and I like it.

The point here is simple. Teach your children everything you know, provide advice when you can, and then support them and watch them grow.

Before I leave the subject of working harder and smarter to become better, realize that most of the A students and most of the F students exist within the 90% I mentioned earlier. Why do some kids get A's and some kids get F's? I came across a study not too long ago that compared the study habits of A, C, and F students. I have used these facts countless times on my own kids and others who happen across my path or attend one of my student presentations. Several thousand students were surveyed in order to understand why similar children (background, ability, circumstance, etc.) sometimes get vastly different grades.

The survey revealed that the primary difference was time spent studying in an organized, effective manner; which translates into working harder and smarter to be better. The survey found that the A student studied on average a minimum of two hours per day, six days a week. Also, the A student studied, for the most part, at the same time, in the same place, under the same conditions. And on days when the A student did not have homework, she would spend time studying anyway. The A student would ask questions of and initiate course material discussions with the teacher. Lastly, the A student studied and did homework with the *objective of understanding the material*.

The C student studied, on average, an hour or less per day, often with no weekend study. Their study locations and time varied somewhat. More often than not, they only studied when there was specific homework due or an upcoming test, and would merely do homework *in order to complete it; contrasted with the student who desired to understand the material* in order to get an A. Furthermore, the C student's contact with the teacher, when it happened at all, was normally initiated by the teacher.

The F student averaged fewer than fifteen minutes per day of homework, and would study with virtually zero continuity of time and location: early morning, late night, on the bus — the F student's "study" time and place was simply all over the board.

So, to my student readers, if you want A's, study like an A student. To the parents of students, please share this with your children.

Of course, motivation to study is the primary reason a person studies. If a student isn't motivated, we all know that the studying won't be that effective. There are many factors that directly affect a student's motivation. I believe the most important reason is the family. However, the point to the survey is this: *once the students determined that they would work at studying, the better grades went to those who studied smarter, longer, and more consistently, using one or more of the practices mentioned above.*

Fantasy High. Earlier, I mentioned that you should visualize success in your chosen field of endeavor. This is healthy and normal, particularly when you have also made the commitment to do the footwork necessary to become successful. A fantasy high, on the other hand, is different. It is also healthy and normal, but over-indulgence could lead to undesirable consequences.

Have you ever bought a lottery ticket? Do you remember your thoughts on the way to buy it? Do you remember how you felt? Do you remember your thoughts as you bought it? Do you remember the fantasy you engaged in after purchase? How long did the fantasy last? How did it make you feel? If you are like most of us, you fantasized about your winnings — what you would buy, how others would view you, how you would feel being rich, and so on. All of these thoughts made you feel good.

I call those thoughts and feelings a *fantasy high*. We all do it. We all enjoy it. Fantasy thoughts of riches, love, sex, power, fame, and heaven (if we are sufficiently drawn to these things) cause you to literally release members of the peptide hormone group (endorphins, dopamine — they resemble the opiates in their ability to produce a feeling of well-being.), and you get high. The drugs make you feel good. Since you are introducing attitude-altering drugs into your system, you must be aware of and careful about how often and how long you use them.

If you have low self-esteem or another type of inferiority complex, fantasy highs can become addictive and therefore immobilizing to the point of being dangerous. If you are a person in a bad relationship, working a job you hate, have children who aren't living up to their potential, and feel that no one really cares for or understands you, you may be using fantasy highs as a way to take the edge off of an otherwise painful and uninspired existence. You might currently use this process as your stress-release mechanism.

In fact, the only time you feel good may be when your thoughts are occupied with fantasies, be they past or future. Past fantasies (whether real, exaggerated, or completely imagined) might be success in high school, sexual conquests, or other experiences that remind you of how good things were before your current relationship, job, or situation devastated your life. Or you might have fantasies of wealth, success, or power to come, after the relationship, job, or other problem-causing circumstance changes. If you begin to dwell on these experiences in order to feel good enough to just get through the day (in other words, use the drugs released during the fantasy high to numb yourself), obvious problems will result. And it is extremely likely that if

——

you are caught in this downward spiral, you will use some other substance (e.g., alcohol and/or drugs) to help trigger the fantasy high. This just makes matters worse.

The point here is to understand that an occasional fantasy high is normal and even healthy (remember, sometimes I *am* Arthur Ashe at Wimbledon); it's the *abuse of fantasy and other highs that is an important and frequent side effect of deeper emotional problems.* The results of such abuse in the career area are often poor job performance, bad attendance, frequent accidents and mistakes, and termination; not to mention the personal and familial problems that could and often do result. As I related in the introduction, I used fantasy highs and other escapes quite extensively while at my low point, prior to my spiritual awakening. These problems are often such that they may require the expertise of a professional to overcome.

Mastery of Habits. I have included a section in this book entitled the "Attributes of Success" which covers some of the habits of successful people I know, have read about, or admire. I also thought it important to discuss the mastery of one's habits in this section. If you plan to do the same job in the same fashion for the rest of your life, please ignore this section. If you intend to excel at your chosen career or do well in your transitional job until you can attack your career, and are interested in making the other material aspects of your life comfortable for you and your loved ones — I'm speaking to you.

Professional reading. Spend at least thirty minutes per day, everyday, reading articles, publications, stories, books, manuals — anything that has anything to do with your profession. You must know what's new, what's old, what's in, what's out, and who is doing what to

97

excel. Change is the only constant in life and business. You must keep abreast of the relentless change that is affecting your business.

In order to improve my financial market presentation ability, knowledge, and delivery, I average reading one business-related book per month. I also read biographies, social commentaries, and pleasure books. In total, I read about 30 books a year. Some of my favorite recent ones are: *Team of Rivals* by Doris Kearns Goodwin; *Guns, Germs and Steel* by Jared Diamond; Harry Dent's *The Roaring 2000's Investor*; Joe Griffith's *Speaker's Library Of Business Stories, Anecdotes and Humor*; Charles Kindleberger's *Manias, Panics, and Crashes*; and *Simple Justice* by Richard Kluger. I also review the staple periodicals of my industry on a daily basis. I actively try to gain knowledge to excel at what I do. Reading helps give me knowledge to do that. What do you read to help you excel in your field? How many books do you read per month?

Financial strategy and leverage. Learn what financially savvy people do with their money, and then do it with yours. Do you have a "free" but zero-interest checking account? Money-wise people don't. They are always attempting to make money with their money, even if it's the bill-paying money. People with money use financial tools such as interest-bearing accounts (i.e., money market) as bill-paying vehicles. They attempt to make money on their money up to the second that the check clears.

Look at your credit cards. What are the interest rates? The major barometer of the stock market, the S&P 500 (This is an economic-size-weighted index of 500 of the largest companies. After the Dow Jones Industrial Average, the S&P 500 is the most widely-followed index of the stocks of large companies. It is considered a bellwether for the American economy.) has gained about 10% annually from 1926 through 2009. Many folks have credit cards with large balances that are charging upwards of 15%. It's hard to make money if you are bringing in ten but spending fifteen.

Furthermore, you only need one or two credit cards. Work to reduce your interest rates on your most established credit cards, and then cancel and cut-up the rest.

Do you maximize your 401(k) or other employer-sponsored retirement plan? Imagine this: you give me a dollar, I add a dollar to it, and then I invest both dollars in the stock market in a tax-deferred account in your name. I also allow you to give me up to 3% of your salary with which I do the exact same thing. On top of that, I allow you to deduct the dollars that you give me from your annual income for tax purposes. Is that cool or what? It is cool, and it's basically how a 401(k) works. Most companies and non-profit organizations offer 401(k)s to their employees.

Most of you reading this are in some type of employer-sponsored plan. If you are, make sure that you have the funds allocated based on your investment tolerance and profile. (All of the major brokerage houses have websites that allow you to run your investor profile without charge.) Specifically, are you a moderate, conservative, or aggressive investor? Once you assess your style and profile, apply it to your 401(k) investments, brokerage accounts, bank accounts, and other assets. Important note: Make sure to view all of your investments as one big pie. Apply your tolerance and profile to the entire pie in order to insure that your investments as a whole reflect your wishes.

And, of course, maximize the amount of your contribution. Most medical experts believe that people in their 40's now, due to medical advances to come, will live well into their 90's. If they are correct, many of us will spend about thirty years in retirement. Most financial experts also say that you will need at least 80% of your current salary to live in the style you are accustomed to while in retirement. So here are the hypothetical numbers for a person now in her forties, making $50,000 per year, who will retire at 65 and live to age 90:

$50,000 x 80% = $40,000 needed per year while in retirement

$40,000 x 25 years = $1,000,000 total needed for 25 years of retirement

For those of you who qualify for a 401(k) but are not maximizing your use of the best investment vehicles around, you must not be aware of it or you don't like money. Consider all of the above, contact your benefits department, and enroll today.

Do you have a brokerage account? Do you know the "Rule of 72"? Here's what it is and how it works. The Rule of 72 is a quick way to calculate how long it takes to double your money at a given interest rate. You simply divide the projected rate of return into 72. For example, let us assume that the current savings account earns 2.0% in interest. How long would it take for you to double $1,000 at this rate?

72/2.0 = 36 years to turn $1,000 into $2,000

Earlier, we mentioned that the stock market, specifically the S&P 500, has averaged around 10.0% since 1926. Let's run it through the rule:

72/10.0 = 7.20 years to turn $1,000 into $2,000

That's 36 years at 2%, versus 7.2 years at 10%.

So the question is a simple one: *How long do you want to wait for your money to double?* **Please note: I am not predicting the financial future, and past performance does not guarantee future results;** however, people in the financial knowledge loop have brokerage accounts which utilize various investment vehicles in order to maximize their potential return. Oh, they might have a small amount of funds at the lower returns, but (depending on their investment tolerance, profile, and timeline) normally not a large amount. Affluent people do not want their money sitting around idle. The lesson here? Follow them and follow their practices with their money.

Do you have adequate insurance coverage? One of the quickest ways to develop an estate for your heirs is through the purchase of insurance. Why? Because if you don't amass a fortune before you die, you can still make sure their needs are met. One of the cheapest forms of life insurance is offered by your company. It's called group term insurance. Look at your circumstances (age, single, married, with children), consider your needs (life, health, disability, long-term care), consult a professional (agents, brokers, the web), consider the various type of coverage available in your area of interest (life, term, whole, variable, universal, etc.), and then make the appropriate decision.

Let's take this process step by step, for example, life insurance: purchase coverage worth at least five times your annual income, if possible, under your employer's group life insurance plan. For pennies on the dollar, you could have an immediate estate worth hundreds of thousands of dollars for your family if something happens to you. If your income allows, look at securing some type of permanent, non-employer-provided individual insurance. This insurance stays in effect as long as you pay your premium whether you are working or not. Contrast that with employer group life insurance which expires when you leave the company. This is important for many reasons. Odds are that you will have several jobs before you retire or pass on, and you don't want your family to be caught without insurance. In addition, private insurance is age and health-based; so (in general), the younger and healthier you are when you apply, the lower cost.

Go through the same process regarding health, vision, disability, and long-term care insurance: get as much as you can of your employer's discounted employee group coverage; then go to private insurers for the rest. Again, please be sure that you keep the private insurance current.

Do you have an estate plan? An estate plan traditionally has four components: a will, a trust, a durable power of attorney and a medical directive. These documents as a group will help you and your family answer such questions as: Who gets what when I pass on? How will my family know my wishes? Who will be executor? Who will be the trustee? Will the process be public? What type of medical care will I receive if I am unable to communicate?

Without these documents, all of these questions will still be answered, but the answers will be provided by parties (courts, judges, lawyers, health care professionals, other relatives) who may not be familiar with or legally bound to carry out your wishes. Let's take a quick look at each. *Please consult a licensed professional for the current laws and relevant details about each document and the regulations in your particular state and how these documents would apply to your specific circumstance. In addition, the potential tax benefits and liabilities of each document should be thoroughly explored prior to making any decision.* Below is the overview of each document in California as of this writing.

Will. This document, also called a testament, gives legal effect to your wishes with respect to disposal of your property upon your death. You need a witness to sign and date the will if it is typewritten. If you prepare your will holographically, meaning handwritten completely by you the author, a witness is not required. In short, a will tells the world who gets your stuff.

Primary advantage of having a will: You are able to state, in advance, what you want to happen with your possessions when you pass.
Primary disadvantage(s): A will goes through probate, which is a public process of settling your affairs, and therefore becomes part of your city's public record. You might also have negative tax consequences.

Trust. A relationship where you select someone to hold title to your property for the benefit of another. The person holding your property has a fiduciary (literally meaning holding something for another) relationship with you. The holding person is the trustee; you, the property owner, are the trustor. The person who will be the future owner is the beneficiary (e.g., your child). You can make the trust irrevocable (you can't change your mind and therefore change the trust) or revocable (you can change it).

Primary advantage of having a trust: as a private transfer of your assets, it avoids probate, and therefore it is normally not part of the public record.

Primary disadvantage(s): it is a legal document that typically requires the assistance and expense of legal and tax professionals. The irrevocable and revocable options have clear and distinct legal and tax implications that may or may not be advantageous for you.

Durable power of attorney. You (principal) appoint another person (agent) to act on your behalf (e.g., for payment of expenses, purchase decisions, the affairs of life.). Durable powers of attorney remain in effect even if you become incompetent. If it is not durable, the power of attorney terminates when or if you are unable to manage your affairs.

Primary advantage of a durable power of attorney: someone will be able to handle your bills and maintain your affairs when you can no longer do it for yourself.

Possible disadvantage: the possibility that you will choose a party who, for whatever reason, is not qualified or able to act effectively on your behalf.

Medical directive (living will, health care proxy). This allows you to establish specific medical care and final wish instructions to those providing care for you; e.g., do you want your family to pull the plug if you are diagnosed as brain dead? Do you wish to be resuscitated if recovery means remaining extremely sick and in pain?

Primary advantage of a medical directive: you can specify how you are to be cared for in what may be your final days.

Possible disadvantage: you choose a party who, for whatever reason, is not qualified to act effectively on your behalf.

These instruments are crucial documents that legally speak to the world on your behalf when you are no longer able to. Again, please *consult a local professional for specific details regarding how these documents may apply to your individual circumstance.*

Do you own real estate? All financially successful people I have ever known, ever read about, ever watched on television—owned real estate. It is simply one of the tickets that you have to get punched as you acquire financial security. Once you are able to stabilize your major monthly expense (for most people, it is rent or mortgage), you are able to budget more effectively. If your biggest expenditure is rent, the amount goes up periodically. If it's a mortgage, it normally tends to remain the same month after month, unless you are in an adjustable mortgage. As you increase your income over time, as most folks do, you end up with more discretionary income with which to pay off debts quicker, accumulate wealth, and spend on wants as well needs. One of the most attractive aspects of real estate is using equity from refinancing to free-up funds for other activity. Also, the tax advantages for most folks may be in the thousands of dollars.

Do you have income property? One of the best ways to legally leverage OPM (other people's money) is to have them buy a property for you. It's called collecting rent. It's a beautiful concept. If you are in it, you know. If you are not, just imagine buying a house, renting it to a tenant, and then being able to legally write off on your taxes the entire mortgage payment, principle, and interest. Imagine writing off every repair from carpet to air conditioning to kitchen remodeling. Imagine writing off every time you visit the property. Well, these are some of the potential tax benefits available to income property owners. If you can't afford to right now, still look into it; you might be surprised. Does your car make you appear wealthier than you are? Get the nice car *after* you get the nice house and income property. It will be worth the wait.

What are your tax write-offs? Some may come from owning income property, owning your own business (even those multi-level marketing businesses), work-related expenses (including tools, education, publications, and additional training), having and raising children. There are many, many other tax advantages. As you know, I am not a licensed tax accountant by training or experience; but for the last few years, I've ordered and used (for free) "*Publication 17, Your Federal Tax Return – For Individuals*" from the Internal Revenue Service while doing my own taxes. It is great document and fairly easy to follow. It tells you the secrets. There are legal ways to reduce your taxes. Take absolute and full advantage of them. Wealthy people do, or have people do it for them. Remember, follow the money.

Credit. Many of the financial tips above require not only your personal funds, but also the use of OPM. In order to obtain the maximum OPM to fulfill your dreams and desires, you need good credit. For the big money, there's no way around it. If you are A-1, you know the feeling. If you are at the other end, you know *that* feeling too, albeit a different and less desirable one. There are agencies and groups around that can help you improve your credit.

Contact them, make the commitment and, most importantly — do the work. Note: Don't get me wrong. I've definitely had my share of tax *and* credit challenges, for that matter. I am sharing with you what I have learned on my journey. A large portion of the learning came through personal, gut-wrenching trial and error; but it was worth it to get to the road I am on now. Again, FLB is about living better everyday by using not only the talents we have, but also the resources available to us.

Be a smart shopper. Check the prices. Compare the values. My dad was a great shopper and would always check prices *anytime* he spent *any* money. He would try to negotiate a better price from the sales clerk at Macy's. I was just a fair shopper. That is to say, I would check most prices and consider things like price per ounce before making a purchase.

But thanks to my wife Linda, I have become a better value shopper, not just a low price shopper.

A few years ago, Linda and I were out and about. We happened upon a sports shoe sale. I found a pair that I liked for about forty bucks that normally would have been ninety or so. I was about to purchase them when she said, "You really like those, don't you?" I said yes. "Why don't you get two, since you like them and they are at such a good price?" I said, "Yeah. That makes sense." Now I always buy at least two pair when I find tennis shoes that I like on sale. For me, last year's model is just fine. As they close out the prior year's stock, shoes that sold for over $100.00 sell for less than $50.00 a pair. When I come across a pair that I like and can play tennis in, I buy two. In addition to the obvious dollar savings, it takes time to find another deal and go make the purchase. I now incorporate how I value my time into the purchase decision, along with the economic value and price.

From houses to food to gas to clothes to vacations: having these things requires spending money. *Your* money and OPM. You've worked hard for it. It often costs to use it. Be smart when parting with it.

Personal. Take care of your house, your car, your gear. Regular recommended tune-ups and oil changes, as-needed house painting, plumbing repair, and general upkeep and maintenance of your environment are all crucial to your overall well-being. When you come home and click the light switch, you don't want to wonder if the bill is paid or if the electrical system works or if this burned-out bulb is the one you said you were going to replace, do you? What you simply want for your family is for the light to come on again and again and again. If there comes a time when it doesn't come on, you take care of it right then (because you keep spares in the house) or do it with urgency in a reasonable period of time.

Now, I am not perfect, and am not claiming that I fix everything the day it breaks or wears out; but it is a goal of mine, when practical. I have also learned to keep several flashlights in the house. We now have an emergency kit, spare bulbs for most lights in our home, and I routinely replace our air filters and check our smoke detectors.

Peace of mind comes from knowing that your car is going to start when your wife and kids are driving home on a raining night after basketball practice; and when you receive your DMW renewal notice, you know that you paid that parking ticket in a timely manner, and kept penalties from being added to your renewal cost.

Also, if you delay too long on any of these things — cars, the front door lock, a dripping faucet, a bad circuit breaker — they may not only cost much more money, but in the end, may be dangerous to you and your family.

Lastly, how can you tell your children to handle their business in school, clean their rooms, and do their chores — in other words be professional — and have them believe it is the right thing to do if *your* bedroom is dirty, you get speeding tickets, and your car blows a head gasket due to neglect? When they are young children, they will do what you say because they have to; but as they get older and are able to control their own destinies, they often will do what they saw you do, not what they heard you say.

Study successful people. Read their books. Watch the biography shows. Try to see them as they are: *people who have been able to harness the resources of the universe (spiritual, physical, material) towards the accomplishment of their goal*. Note that truly successful people tend to watch less television, read more, and sleep less. They tend to be less involved with gossip, hearsay, and conjecture in the areas of human frailty. They tend to be positive, concept-based, optimistic individuals. Successful people tend to encourage others. They act as if they know and understand the positive universal law of karma: if you do good for good's sake, good will come to you. More on this in "Attributes of Success" later.

As a presenter and college professor, I try to hear a good speaker every week. Business presentations, CSPAN, recognition and awards ceremonies, even church are all opportunities for me to see how others do what I do for a living, and to learn from them.

Accept it and love it, or change it to love it. If you are a bus driver (or whatever it is you do) and you *want* to be a bus driver, then be the best, most professional bus driver you can be. We need great bus drivers. We need great, reliable, responsible people in all professions. Accept your career. Thank the force for blessing you with the ability to do what you do; and look forward with anticipation to every day that you have the opportunity to do it, and do it well. No complaints, no regrets, no whining — you are lucky enough to do what you said you want to do. Get to work.

Conversely, if you don't want to do what you are doing, then that becomes your transitional job. Do it well while actively preparing (with the steps we discussed earlier, including visualizing, not fantasizing) for your next career. Again, no complaints, no regrets — just get to work on the next step; and thank the spirit daily for the gift of a transitional job that allows you to prepare for the next step in your career while your bills are still being paid. Get to work.

Do you see it? By employing *Full Life Balance* to your professional life, you become either busy being good at what you do, or busy preparing for what you truly want to do while temporarily doing (with a positive, thankful attitude) what you don't want to do. That's all there is. It's that simple. There isn't time for the distractions, resentments, and fantasies of the unfulfilled and misguided. You are too involved in what you are trying to achieve: complete professional success. It's like,

"Sorry, guys, I can't participate in the 'We hate this job ritual' in the lunchroom today, because I've got some positive work to do." Get to work.

THE FIVE PROFESSIONAL SECRETS

1. Know that it is not just *what* we do or *how* we do it or *why* we do it or *how much we get paid* to do it or *how much* we enjoy it — it's all of these things. They are all connected.
2. Identify the thing that you are gifted to do.
3. Work harder and smarter to become better at your gift.
4. Apply the "Work harder and smarter" adage to your entire life.
5. Develop mastery of your personal and professional habits.

The Spiritual Key

"Why aren't you dancing with joy at this very moment?" is the only relevant spiritual question. – Pir Vilayer Khan

I believe that the most important key of *Full Life Balance* is the spiritual one. Simply, it is to acknowledge that there is something greater than we are. To live your life as an acknowledgement that there is an omnipotent, omnipresent, positive force, *and* know and respect the existence of a very powerful negative force.

There are three levels of human understanding: first, the mental or intellectual level; second is the religious or the devotional level; and the third and deepest level is the personal or experiential level. An example of understanding on the mental level is how most of us know and believe that the earth is round. Most of us have never flown around the world or viewed it from space to actually witness the spherical shape, but we believe it because we have been told by what we consider qualified sources. The intellectual issue with this level of belief is that one has to accept the contention of an outside source because, in many cases, one will never be able to personally verify the facts.

An example of the second or devotional level is how millions of people believe that Jesus Christ was crucified and rose from the grave. Many who believe this would not normally accept the resurrection as intellectual fact; but because of their faith or devotion, they believe with the very fiber of their being that it happened. In fact, many are willing to bet their lives on it. The problematic issue with devotional belief is that you have to continually fight the illogic of many beliefs (many experts agree that most human minds are logical, even if we don't always act logically) with the rational part of the mind. One has to override logic by bullying one's mind and saying things like, "That's just what I believe. I have faith."

The third type of belief is based on personal eyewitness experience, the experiential level. Look at your personal knowledge of fire. At some point in your early childhood you learned the characteristics of fire. You learned that fire burns. You learned this lesson, *not* because your parents kept saying, "Don't touch that— it's hot, hot, hot." You didn't initially understand "hot." You *learned* hot for yourself when you touched the stove or the heater's hot surface and then *felt* the burn. When you felt that sensation, you learned in the very core of your being that fire was hot, hot enough to hurt.

Once you learned it in this way, you would never have to "learn" it again. This is personal, experiential learning. Many experts in the study of the mind contend that the third or experiential learning level is the most effective and most permanent type of understanding. We all carry beliefs based on all three levels. Some things we take for fact, some things we just believe, and others we actually experience.

So, how can you know in the very fiber of your being, at the third level of understanding, that there is an omnipotent, omnipresent positive force? Many books, publications, and religious and spiritual people have their well-publicized opinions and philosophies on the subject. I suggest you search to find the way that works best for you. It would be great if, after reading this section, you were totally convinced of the ALL powerful spirit in the way I am, in the very fiber of my being. That would be nice, but I don't expect it to happen from *just* reading this book.

What I hope will happen, for those who don't currently believe, is that I might help you consider the possibilities as you search for your own spiritual truth. For those who do believe, I hope this section helps deepen your understanding.

That being said, here's what worked and is working for me. Initially, as I mentioned earlier, I had a spiritual epiphany. This experience was obviously at the third level of understanding — the personal, experiential level. It happened to *me*. While in the pit of personal despair, I cried out for help; and the request was unequivocally answered and I was changed. As a result of this change, I have zero doubt as to the existence and ability of the universal spirit. If you are in the pit of emotional, physical, or psychological despair, do what I did: cry out for help. Ask the spirit to save you. I asked; and as a result of my epiphany, my life and my effect on those around me were altered dramatically for the better.

Some scientists, agnostics (someone who believes it is not possible to know whether God exists or not) and atheists (someone who believes God does not exist) contend that the root causes of spiritual epiphanies and other personal spiritual phenomena can be traced to certain types of personal, emotional, psychological and/or environmental trauma. The essence of their position is that the human brain often creates the appropriate response to the request for help if, among other factors, that request is intense enough. Following this line of thought, they may claim that I was so intense in my desire to change my life that I, essentially, changed my life from within in response to my urgent and desperate request for help. To those folks, I politely and respectfully say, OK. If, while in my personal trauma, I called on some force and that force responded, but that force was within me all along, not some external power, I simply say, OK. I'll take most of that with one modification: I believe the force to be universal. I believe it permeates everything. It is external and internal.

Next, I began to consistently do three things. First, I made a conscious choice and effort to seek the positive force. Second, I began to strive daily through my thoughts and actions to live my life as an example of the peace, contentment, joy, and perspective that will be bestowed on all who actively seek the blessings of the positive force. One of my daily prayers became the statement/question, "Now that you've saved me, what would you have me do?" Third, I strove diligently to avoid the mind (ego) and body (sensual) traps frequently laid in my path by the negative force. Many religious and spiritual people testify that if you do these steps consistently, even without an epiphany, you can reach spiritual awareness and, hopefully, enlightenment.

How can you know that there is a very powerful negative force? Well, just watch the news. We are all blessed with the gift of will, the gift of choice. We can clearly (and in the overwhelming majority of cases, knowingly) choose to do right or wrong: we can decide to do good or bad. As long as we have the gift of choice, some of us will choose evil. The evidence of the good essence, spirit, or force, as well as the evidence of the bad, is all around us.

Earlier, I listed some of the various names we use to refer to the spirit. I apologize, with all sincerity, to any and all true worshipers of the spirit if I have not included the name you prefer to use when you call on the force of your understanding. But I believe that the source *doesn't care what you call it*. The issue is not what you call it; the important issue is *whether or not you call on it*.

I am part Christian, part Muslim, part Buddhist, part Jehovah's Witness, part Seventh-Day Adventist, and on and on. In short, I am part of and support any and all religions when the doctrines and the followers advocate peace and understanding, and seek goodness. I am not part of any religion whose doctrine (or its followers' interpretation of the doctrine) does not advocate peace and understanding, and seek goodness. I am simply a believer and a seeker.

You can achieve *Full Life Balance* and not necessarily believe what I believe. You can be Christian, Buddhist, Hindu, Muslim, or a spiritual seeker of any other religious or spiritual persuasion, and still achieve *Full Life Balance*. *Full Life Balance* suggests that part of your life be devoted to the pursuit of true, honest, and personal spiritual awareness and enlightenment, however you achieve it.

I don't profess to have all the answers. *But I have found, through study, conversation and inquiry, that the essence of goodness is in every true religion.* I don't think my spiritual beliefs trump your beliefs, assuming yours are focused on the natural and honest quest for true spirituality. I think that the essence of true spirituality can be summed up in the following statement: do good, be good, and show others, by your example, the power of goodness. If you choose not to define your spiritual life the way I define mine, I not only contend that it is your right to do so, but I will defend your right to do so.

However, whatever your concept of spirituality is, I pray that it has something to do with doing good, being good, and showing others, by your example, the power of goodness. If it is, we all benefit. If it's not, well... history is full of examples of the destructive power of misguided, twisted religious belief and spiritual misinterpretation. I believe we should contemplate a way that considers what the spirit would truly want. Would the spirit want religious wars? Would the true spirit want conversion by threat, force or bloodshed? Does that make spiritual sense?

With many religions that practice strict, dictatorial dogma, the age-old question presents itself: "How do you know with absolute certainty that your way is right and *all other ways are wrong*?"

What do you worship? The *American Heritage Dictionary* defines worship as "...a) reverent love and devotion for a deity or sacred object; b) ardent devotion, adoration." What are you devoted to? What do you adore? Someone once said, in essence, "Tell me what you love, and I'll tell you what you are." You need to look inside yourself on a regular basis and examine what drives you, what you are devoted to, what motivates you, and what you worship in order to understand what you truly are.

This search, this need to understand what we are, has caused human kind to contemplate the existence of something greater than ourselves. In my life, I have been blessed to be able to confirm that existence. And by that confirmation, the spirit has altered the course of my history, my present, and my future. Once I made not only the confirmation but also an intimate connection with something greater than I, another funny thing happened—I began to gain **spiritual life perspective**.

Part of spiritual life perspective is to know that right now, this very moment as you read this book, is the most important moment of your life. It's not yesterday's news or tomorrow's challenge; it is right now. That's right. The most important moment in your life is right now. It is *living* your actions right now; it is living as if your next conversation could be your very last. That doesn't mean you don't make plans for the future and it doesn't mean you neglect the lessons and memories of the past. It means you should live your life as if today's sunset could be your final one. If you knew that, oh, how you would treasure the colors and emotions that something as beautiful as a sunset stirs inside of you.

I saw a movie once about a man who was going deaf. He began to travel through his daily life literally collecting sounds. He went to the railroad track to hear a train; he stood outside his neighbor's door to listen to her singing; he called his daughter to listen to her voice on the phone. We all face one common, chilling, certain reality: sometime after physical birth, there is physical death. The only temporal questions are 1) how will we live and, 2) how and when will we die. Spiritual life perspective *is being right here right now and enjoying it.* It is waking up on Monday and being really, really glad you *awoke, not annoyed that it is Monday.*

I meet people all the time, and I'll ask, "How are you?" If it's Monday, you probably know the most frequent reply: something to the effect that either the weekend was too short; or, here we go again; or something equally worthless, negative, and mentally destructive. If I query on a day other than Monday (but not Friday or the weekend), most often I'll hear, "It's just another day in the grind…I'm not too bad…As well as can be expected…A day closer to Friday," and the like. If I happen to inquire on a Friday, I normally receive the usual TGIF-type of statements. So, the typical week unfortunately for many is essentially:

> "Oh my GOD, it's **Monday**."

> **Tuesday** — "A day closer to Wednesday."

> **Wednesday** — "Hump day; we're half way there."

> **Thursday** — "I can coast now because tomorrow is…"

> **Friday** — "Oh, I've waited all week for this day."

> **Saturday** — "Boy, that went fast."

> **Sunday** — "Well, back to the grind tomorrow…."

> "Oh my GOD, it's **Monday.**"

If you are one of the unfortunate people on this treadmill, you are *anticipating* living (if living is enjoying your life and the day you've been given) two-and-one-half days per week. In fact, if you are on this miserable toll road, no day is actually *lived*. Each day is spent in anticipation or dread of the blessed but not promised next day. And the toll taken from you on this road is

119

incredibly high — a day of your life you will never see again. What a way to live. *What an awful and costly way to live.*

I hope this example isn't characteristic of how you live and view your days. If it isn't, congratulations. Continue doing whatever it is you're doing that has allowed you to gain perspective, hopefully a spiritual life perspective. However, if it *is* how you view your days, then just imagine changing your life to the point where you awake everyday fired up, excited and thankful. Be it Monday, Wednesday, Friday or Saturday. Just imagine.

That's how I wake up. That's how millions awaken. It is one of the greatest gifts of *Full Life Balance*: **a spiritual life perspective.**

Life is dynamic, full of ebbs and flows. Likewise, we — our bodies, our minds, and our spirits — are dynamic. We need to invigorate, maintain, and replenish our bodies, our minds and our spirits. Later, we'll discuss ideas to invigorate, maintain and replenish our physical and mental selves. Spiritually, there are many things we can do to enhance and maintain our spirituality; in short, to raise our level of spiritual consciousness. And here again, the best way is the way that works best for you. Here are some of the things that work well for me: **prayer, meditation, and seeking the light in life.**

Prayer. The *American Heritage Dictionary* defines prayer as "a reverent petition made to deity" or "a fervent request." Prayer is our attempt at direct, conscious communication with the universal spirit.

Why pray? I wish I could explain it, but something special happens when you open your heart and mind and *ask something greater than yourself for help. Something answers. Not always on your timetable, but something answers; not always based on your understanding; but something answers. Just pray.*

When should you pray? Pray everyday. Pray as often as you want to. Pray as often as you need to. Pray when you're scared. Pray when you're happy. Pray when you're thankful. Pray by yourself. Pray in a room full of people. Pray at the red light. Pray in the bathroom. Pray after a good serve, basket, or point. Pray before, during and after a meal. Pray when you study for, take, pass, or even fail a test. Just pray.

Pray to whom? To the good. To the spirit. To God. To Allah. To the source. To the force that permeates everything. Just pray. How to pray? With your eyes closed. With you eyes open. On your knees. Standing up. Lying down. Pray with your thoughts. Pray with your voice. Just pray. What to pray? Ask the spirit to help you be the person it wants you to be. Pray for forgiveness. Pray to be nicer. Pray to be better. Pray to be kinder. Pray for your family, friends, animals — the world. Pray for understanding, patience and hope. Give thanks.

Here is a sample prayer: "Thank you for my hand. Thank you for the miracle of being able to write. Pick things up. Pat my daughter on the head. Guide food to my face. Let me grow to be the person you would have me be and always use my hand for good."

Just pray and be thankful.

Meditation. Time without distraction is important for you. You need peace and time daily to hear what the inner you is saying. If you awake to an alarm clock; turn on the TV or radio; talk to family as they and you prepare for the day; hop in the car and turn on music; get to work; interact with computers, people, machines and such; go eat lunch with or around people and possibly more music; get back to work; hop in the car, turn on the music, news, or sports talk; do an after-work errand or two; interact with more people; get home; interact with family; eat; watch TV; and finally go to bed; then when do you have actual quiet time? When do you have uncluttered, undistracted *you on you* time? All the things you do daily are important, and many *must* be done; but you are the most important thing you have, and what goes on inside of you needs to be heard and reflected upon. Meditation is great way to secure this quiet time.

"To reflect on; to contemplate" is to meditate. Why meditate? There are many good reasons and opinions. For me, meditation helps develop a deeper understanding of who I am, what I feel, what I believe, and why I do what I do. It replenishes me. It helps me become grounded. It helps me release some of the stresses and strains of the day. I recently returned from a meditation retreat.

Similar to yet vastly different from prayer, meditation helps you get more in touch with your inner self, your feelings, and your spirit. Through meditation you enhance your contact with and knowledge of your spirit, and you can develop a fuller understanding of yourself and your actions. It is a very private and internal activity, but its effects radiate from you. In meditation you aren't asking, you aren't telling, you aren't thanking; you are just being and enjoying being and contemplating being.

There are various ways to meditate and various types of meditation. Most people have the ability to meditate alone. Others may need help. If you use the assistance of a facilitator, seek one that teaches neutral meditation. "Neutral" in this sense means the type of meditation without a philosophy attached. Simply put, I suggest seeking pure meditation, uncluttered by doctrine or dogma; meditation for the sake of meditation in order to get in touch with your personal truth.

I don't claim to be an expert on this vast subject, but I will share with you some of the things I learned as I began to use it in my life. First, how do you meditate?

One of the most important things I seek is a peaceful location. I like to meditate in a distraction-free environment. I find a place of relative silence. I like to meditate while sitting comfortably in a chair, but sometimes I sit on the floor (some opt for lying down; whatever works best for you). Once the location is peaceful, I close my eyes and begin to relax and clear my mind.

The goal at this point is to shut down the normal daily clutter in my mind and to decrease the impact of all other thought in order to allow my total consciousness to focus simply on meditation. I like to imagine a lake with lots of rippling waves. Each wave represents a challenge or concern. I try to imagine my eyes at water level. As I look across the lake, I begin to calm each wave (challenge or concern), thereby reducing its power to distract. At this moment these concerns aren't important. They have no power over my thought or need any immediate action. I am not trying to think about them in the context of solving them at this moment. As I focus on each wave, reducing them, eliminating their power, the lake becomes tranquil.

As the lake becomes tranquil, I become tranquil. From this point, I can choose to direct my consciousness to various areas of my mind, body, and spirit. For example, I can simply focus on the miracle of my heartbeat. I can focus on the fact that my heart beats, right on time, all the time, everyday. Effortlessly, relentlessly, my heart beats to pump blood, and I live. Sometimes my meditation consists of five to fifteen minutes of peace and quiet. Sometimes, I sit and just let my self and my spirit speak to me without distraction.

When to meditate? I try to meditate at least once daily for a minimum of five minutes, usually in the evening; but recently, I have begun to meditate in the morning. It's a nice way to start the day. Again, I suggest you try various combinations of time of day, length of time, and frequency to determine what meditation routines work best for you. Another simple suggestion: in addition to daily regular meditation, when you feel like meditating, do it. Do it as often as you like.

Seeking the light in life. Look for the good. I try not to watch the nightly who-killed-whom-news. Constantly filling yourself with the daily testimony of the depths of human depravity can only make you feel paranoid, jaded and less human. I'm not saying you should be unaware of your environment; there is evil in the world, and you should take the necessary precautions to care for yourself and others. But to continuously remind yourself in graphic detail how much evil there is can't be good for your mental, emotional or spiritual self.

You should seek out the "good news." When you hear, see, think, do, and/or feel something good, positive and enlightening, you should revel in, treasure and spread it. This will help you feel confident, optimistic and more human. Conversely, you should avoid like the plague things *and* people that are bad, negative, destructive, and dehumanizing.

Often, the last thing I see at night is Linda's loving face, or the pages of a good book, or something that makes me laugh. The last thing I think at night will normally be a prayer or idea that helps me accomplish something I'm focused on. I believe if I give my mind good, positive "food" to digest overnight, I can't help but manifest positive energy when I awake the next day.

When "seeking the light in life," you need not look far. All around you, everyday, there are numerous examples of the works of the good, beautiful, positive force. You just have to open your ears, eyes, mind, and spirit to become aware of and appreciative of the goodness and beauty around you. Just observe *any* baby (human or animal) doing *anything,* and you will know what I mean. Go to the ocean and just watch the waves come in and go out, over and over and over again. You'll begin to appreciate the miracle and enhance your perspective.

A couple of years after I became spiritually aware and spiritually connected, I made a surprising discovery. I was a stockbroker at a large investment firm, working in an office in San Mateo, California. One nice spring day — the sun was shining, a slight breeze was blowing — I went out the front door and was literally hit with the most incredible fragrance. I asked what the aroma was, and someone said it was star jasmine. At the time I was 40 years old. This was the first time I had consciously been aware of the fragrance of star jasmine.

This was amazing to me. I had been on the planet for over 14,600 days. I had experienced forty springs and summers, nineteen as an adult. I was college-educated. I had been married. I had teenaged children. I had managed the careers of a large number of employees. And I had never consciously taken the time to smell star jasmine before. Wow, what a fragrance. More importantly, what a revelation. I called Linda (at the time my fiancée) and described the aroma I had just experienced. She was surprised, in fact a little amazed, that I had never noticed star jasmine before.

What else had I been missing? I realized, through the hustle and bustle of my teenage and college years, through the rigorous demands of my early career and raising a family, through the years of my downward spiral, and then through the uplifting years after my awakening, that I had always been very busy. And even then, at age 40, while I was growing in a number of areas, I still might have been too busy becoming balanced to smell the proverbial roses.

Guess what I do now when I see flowers? I look at them. Sometimes I touch them. I drink them in. I appreciate them. Due to occasional allergies, I can't always smell them, but I have made paying attention to them one of my symbols of active engagement and awareness of the beauty that surrounds me. I try to actively "smell the star jasmine" in my life.

Each day, each month, each year, are simply opportunities for more chances to enjoy the good, more opportunities for revelations. More opportunities to seek out the light in life. And when we expose ourselves to and appreciate the light, it feels good. And it is human nature to be attracted to things that feel good. However, it is also human nature to become bored by experiencing the same types of stimuli again and again; so it follows that in order to stay in the light, we have to constantly seek the light in its various and constantly changing forms. The good news is that there is light all around us.

We just have to open ourselves in order to see and appreciate it.

We should share our spirituality, through our actions, with everyone around us. Helping someone who has fallen down, giving a few dollars or food to a homeless person, passing on a kind and concerned word to someone feeling down—all are ways to show we have the light inside.

Writing this book has helped me look at my own actions on many levels. One of those levels is how my spirituality is interpreted by my children. Our children in particular (and *all* children we come in contact with in general) need demonstrations of and discussions about your and their spirituality. Let me relate something that happened to me recently.

As I mentioned earlier, I have children from an earlier marriage. On most Sundays, I pick them up and we go to church. After church, we normally go to visit my grandmother, whom we call "Gramon." Most of my immediate family drops by Gramon's on Sunday, so this has given the kids time with my side of their family. But back to the story. Initially, I began taking the kids to church on Sundays because I was taken to church on Sundays. In time, I took them because I wanted to be sure they knew that there was something greater than man, and to make sure they knew I believed in it.

We developed a ritual whereby after the services, each of us would have to state the concept that most stuck with us from the service. It was not a big formal deal. During our walk back to car or after we get in, each of us simply reviews the one topic that made the most sense or was the most interesting or was the most difficult to understand. This is how I make sure that they are at least somewhat engaged in what is going on in church. During our debriefing, I often summarize the discussion and add my opinions and thoughts.

About three weeks ago, as I gathered my thoughts for this section of the book, I was preparing to pick up the kids up from their house, and I wondered what my children thought about my spiritual beliefs. I realized that, because I was raised Baptist, out of habit I had only taken them, on our various Sundays, to Baptist and Methodist churches. During our after-church conversations and analyses, however, I did cover other spiritual and religious possibilities.

The contradictory message of these Sunday church outings was that I had told them for years that there was merit in all religions that profess the essential doctrine of "do good, be good, and, by your thoughts and actions, show others the power of goodness." But I had only formally exposed them to essentially one artery of the spiritual body. So, I thought, I need to at least expose them to Buddhism, Hinduism, Islam, Religious Science, and other beliefs so that they could compare, contrast, and conclude for themselves. First, I would have to have a session with them to share my revelation of this oversight with them.

On this particular Sunday, I picked them up and told them, "Today, we are going to the Church of What do You Believe?" They said, "Huh?" We drove to Twin Peaks (which has one of the more beautiful views of the San Francisco skyline and bay), parked, and had one of the most meaningful spiritual discussions I have ever had. I began by apologizing for not exposing them to other religious thoughts and ideas. They were confused at first. I shared what I believed, reviewed what I had told them about seeking their truth through learning and listening to various opinions, and said that it didn't make sense for me to just take them to Baptist and

Methodist institutions.

They agreed, and slowly began to talk about how the pastors of most of the churches we normally go to say basically the same thing, with only a slightly different twist. William II mentioned that sometimes the pastors cover interesting thoughts that stick with him. Tiye agreed, but also said that there probably *are* a lot of opinions and beliefs in the world.

The discussion evolved into a talk on the meaning of life, where we fit in, and what is spiritual truth, among other topics. We also considered and discussed some of the most profound questions known to man: "If there is an all-powerful God, why does He allow such pain and suffering? What is good? What is bad?" and more. We spent nearly three hours having possibly the deepest spiritual discussion of their young lives and mine. We also concluded that we would try a different religious experience when we got together the next Sunday.

Now *that* was a real session of church. Afterward, it was very clear to me that those young people knew that I cared about their minds, bodies, souls, and the quality of their lives; and I understood how important and lasting the lessons of life, spirituality, and beliefs were to them. They had not only remembered what my beliefs were, but they had also taken the time and thought needed to develop and articulate their own. If pride is a sin, I sinned that day. It does make me proud to know that I am affecting them this way.

That's just an example of sharing your spirituality. Of course, you should share your thoughts and demonstrate your beliefs regarding other areas of life with your children as well (we will discuss the other aspects later). Please make sure that they know what you stand for spiritually. The knowledge of what you stand for in thought and in deed will serve them — and you — well for the rest of their lives.

THE FIVE SPIRITUAL SECRETS

This may be the most important stage of *Full Life Balance* is *spiritual*.

1. Develop a spiritual life perspective.
2. Consciously seek the positive source.
3. Strive daily to do good, be good, and, through your thoughts and actions, show others (especially the children) the power of good.
4. Avoid the mind and body traps that lie in your path.
5. Use prayer, meditation, and seeking the light to maintain and enhance your spiritual perspective.

ALL, A prayer

I believe
> *That there is an ALL powerful spirit...which grants life, instills faith, and empowers love.*

I believe
> *That this spirit, which has no sex, no race, no bias, no limitations, has, throughout time, allowed a negative spirit to exist.*

I believe
> *That the ALL powerful spirit does not care what it is called, or what language you pray in, or exactly how you pray...as long as you call upon the spirit from your heart and soul.*

I believe
> *That the ALL powerful spirit has no religious preference, but has revealed itself throughout time to all seekers in various religions...and all seekers outside of religion, with the only prerequisite being the search for spiritual light.*

I believe
> *That our purpose in life is to seek the favor of this all-powerful spirit through prayer, thought, and actions by the use of the gift of will.*

I believe
> *That if we live in the spirit, the spirit reinforces, renews, reinvigorates and replenishes us by allowing us to be more of what the spirit wants us to be: kind, compassionate, healthy, loving, moral, charitable, friendly, directed, and learned.*

I believe

> That the purpose of the negative spirit is to provide the natural "reference points" for all spirit-based behavior and thoughts (you appreciate sunshine more after days and days of rain).

I believe

> That the ALL powerful spirit is exactly that — it is ALL, it controls ALL. ALL gives us free will, which allows us choose the light or the darkness.

> ALL is well.

The Charitable Key

"I wondered why somebody didn't do something; then I realized that I was somebody."- Anonymous

I have been surrounded by people filled with the spirit of generosity for as long as I can remember. Charitable people, activities, and events have enriched and improved my life. I have been tutored, mentored, counseled, coached — in short, helped personally by everyday people who transformed themselves into angels the day they said, "I can help and I will help."

Without the people who spent time with me, paid attention to me, asked me questions, challenged me, disciplined me, and showed that I was important to them, I don't know where I would be. There were thousands and thousands of young men and women who were born around the time I was born, who were born into similar social conditions as me, who now no longer breathe.

There are thousands of others who no longer breathe the air of free men. Why me? And why *did* those like me make it? In addition to our families and the spirit, I believe it was the "volunteer angels" that were sent to guide, protect, and direct us through the maze of youth and young adulthood.

I am willing to bet that you know someone who made it through a Hunters Point, Watts, some sections of Harlem, Marcy Projects, or any of the thousands of other low-income, high-despair housing projects throughout the urban centers of this country. I will always have awe and respect for those of you who walked streets similar to my own and now stand as active, positive, contributing men and women in our society. Another similarity most of us have in common is

133

that someone, in addition to one or both parents, reached down to help us.

Most of us can relate a story of a camp counselor, a volunteer coach, a Sunday school teacher, or even the local barber who said or did something at a pivotal point in our lives to help coax us in the right direction. Most of us feel some type of obligation to do the same for someone else.

However, it does not matter if you experienced a childhood similar to mine, or if a volunteer angel did or did not reach down to help you. You are standing today because of the love and care shown by others to you. Here's hoping that you, too, feel the need to give back. For most of us, time, not intent, is the challenge.

I hope what I relate to you over the next few pages reinforces the volunteer efforts you already participate in; or, for those who aren't involved currently but say you want to, encourages you to begin to allocate the time.

Of course, I have stories. I became aware of the concept of summer camp when I was about ten years old. I somehow found out about how kids could go away for two weeks in the summer, spend time in the woods, and come back with all kinds of stories about different adventures they'd had. I wanted to go, too; but there wasn't money in our family budget, so none of us had ever gone up to that point. Luckily for me and thousands of other kids, there was a group of people who cared. This group donated time, money, and effort to help kids. They sold Christmas trees to raise funds to subsidize families who couldn't afford the luxury of camp. That group was and is the Guardsmen. Because of this group of angels, in the summer of 1967, at the age of twelve, I went to camp for the first time in my life.

It was everything I had hoped for and imagined. I did all the camper stuff: hiking, climbing, horseback riding, telling ghost stories, roasting marshmallows over the campfire, and sleeping under the stars. It still rates in the top ten on the list of my greatest personal experiences. Thank you, men and women of the Guardsmen. You have no idea what you did for me. I will always be in your debt. Also, thank you to the folks who bought Christmas trees from the Guardsmen instead of from someone else. You made the difference.

There was a lady who at age of thirty-one became, as a result of divorce, a single parent with five children under the age of eleven. This lady could have applied for various types of assistance, but she had worked hard raising her children to this point and had become a Licensed Vocational Nurse (LVN). She felt that if she could become a Registered Nurse (RN), she might be able to make enough money to do a little more than just get by. She was blessed with a loving mother and father, and was able to count on them to help watch her kids as she worked full-time, raised her kids full-time, and went to school part-time. Time went by, and this woman met the man who would marry and live the rest of his life loving her. They had a daughter, and then the family totaled eight.

The woman did become an RN. Years later, after an enriched and fulfilled life, she retired from nursing. That same year, she received her Masters in Psychology. She was a practicing family therapist when she passed from this plane of existence ten years later.

That woman was my mother, Mrs. Ora Campbell. The reason I am relating a brief section of her history here (as opposed to including her in the professional section) is that in addition to everything I just mentioned, through it all, she was one of the most active volunteers I have ever witnessed. From teaching Sunday school at church to being a den mother for the Campfire Girls; from tutoring to creating and running the annual Career Fair at the Hunters Point Boys Club; to creating and presiding as president over a chapter of the North Bay Area Continentals: the list just goes on.

Mrs. Ora Campbell spent her life making a difference. There are former Campfire Girls who, as mothers and even grandmothers themselves today, still relate to me and my siblings stories of my mom's kindness, guidance, and compassion when we chance upon them.

From watching her and my experience with the Guardsmen, the Boy's Club, Double Rock Baptist Church, Pete the barber, Ashley the coach, Mrs. Shukamora the sixth-grade teacher, and countless others, I learned that I had to do something to make things better for someone else. I also learned from my mom that I could do quite a few charitable activities simultaneously.

As we view the state of our country (for that matter, the world), if we are thinking, feeling humans, we must draw one inescapable conclusion: we must do something. I believe that we can't just get a good education, a great job or career, work as if we are possessed to acquire the trappings of affluence, and then call it a day. Go ahead and get those things. Enjoy those things. But I believe that too many people went before us to pave the road we now walk on; and the toll they often paid was their lives. The least we can do is give some of our time.

Education for you and your family, jobs, and economic security are important and have their place. You and I *have* earned the right to have baubles, trinkets, and such. I know that being financially, socially, and vocationally successful does not necessarily obligate you to help your fellow humans; but it does enable you to make a bigger, positive impact with less sacrifice.

You may only be able to give time. You may be able to only give money. You may be blessed with the ability to give both time and money. Helping someone other than your family (and friends) and being successful aren't mutually exclusive concepts. We can do both. We can have these things and still do something to help change the world for the better.

Crack babies, fatherless young boys, the emotionally disturbed, pregnant teens, the homeless, the desperate and desolate, sick and shut-ins, the ecology — there are too many causes to mention. Take your pick. There's a cause for everyone. Too many needs are unfulfilled. Can you do an hour a week being a big brother or reading to an elderly widow? Coaching a girls' softball team? Can you do an hour a month? You choose it. The world needs it, so do it. Consider it a tribute to your ancestors. Consider it a down payment on your future. You might see that young person who needs help again, maybe when he is applying for a job at your company. Maybe it's when he's standing behind your wife shifty-eyed while she's getting money out of the ATM. I opt to help now. Change a life now.

My mom told me that if everyone just volunteered two to three hours a week, we could solve most of the world's problems. I believe her. Can you help? Will you help?

The Stadium Scholarship Program. In 1996 while working as a stockbroker in San Mateo, California, I decided that I would spend one day per week working out of the Oakland office. Oakland is a low- to-moderate-income, largely minority city of about 450,000 persons across the bay from San Francisco. San Mateo is a moderate- to high- income, majority European American city with a population of about 100,000 located about twenty miles south of San Francisco on the peninsula.

While spending one day per week in Oakland, I became active with the Chamber of Commerce and, as a result, was selected for the Leadership Oakland program. (Many cities have these programs. They are designed to indoctrinate potential city leaders into the processes of government through a series of meetings, forums, and question-and- answer sessions with the city's various political, educational, cultural, and social heads.)

We met with, among others, the mayor, members of the city council, the chiefs of police and fire, and the general manager of the port and airport; and had interesting, sometimes testy exchanges as we discussed the status and future of the city.

Midway through the program, we had sports day. It featured representatives from Oakland's three professional sports teams, the Oakland A's, Golden State Warriors, and the Oakland Raiders. As each team made its respective presentation regarding the sports and business aspects of its franchise, a thought kept gnawing at me. I kept thinking about how we were sitting there discussing sports as a business; while for many boys of African descent, it's not just a way of life—in their minds, it's the only future worth living.

Sitting there, I thought about speaking as a school volunteer to boys between the ages of eight and fifteen, and asking what they wanted to be when they grew up. A large percentage of the African American boys laid claim to one vocation: that of a professional athlete (more recently, many say they also want to become rap artists). Most of the European American boys I've spoken to during these sessions aspired to two occupations. One is in sports, but the other was one of the doctor-lawyer-fireman responses.

I thought about how, from kindergarten through the third grade, many boys of African descent do well in school; but something apparently happens around the end of the third grade. Their grades begin to dip.

This is about the time they start wanting to be cool. In their world, it's basketball, football, baseball, rap, and fighting skills that set them apart, make them cool on the playground and in front of their peers. It's not how smart they are or how good their grades are. Of course, some are lucky enough to have parents, coaches, teachers, pastors, and other folks who are actively working to show them the light of opportunity and possibility; and as result, that lucky group has a more rounded and realistic notion of their prospects as adults.

As I mulled this dilemma, a question hit me: What if there was a way to combine the attraction these kids have to sports with the need to reinforce good academics and citizenship? So I addressed the Oakland leaders and talked it through. I spoke about our collective obligation and responsibility as adults and business people. I stressed the importance of doing something to give back to the kids and communities who are making idols out of athletes and religions out of sports. I talked about the targeted marketing of the athletes; their shoes, sport drinks, and glamour that help perpetuate the hero worship at the altars of the NFL, NBA and MLB.

I believe I concluded with something similar to, "What if we could recognize kids for their scholastic achievement and good citizenship, and do it in a 'cool' environment? What if we let the kids march out on mid-court at half-time at a Golden State Warriors game and flash their picture on the big screen so that they can receive the accolades of the fans? Plus, what if we gave them a little money as a reward for their hard work?" Most everyone said that it was a good idea. Then they went back to talking about the business of sports. Two of the folks who agreed with the idea were Mr. David Alioto of the A's and Mr. Al Attles of the Warriors. In fact, former NBA player Attles made the *mistake* of saying that he would work with me on the idea.

So, over the next few weeks, I developed it. We would call it the Stadium Scholarship program (SSP). We would select kids between the ages of eight and twelve from the Oakland Unified School District. I decided that I would cast a net that included boys and girls. Each child would receive a check for $100.00 in their name (we would ask businesses to put up the funds). Each student would receive two tickets and a parking pass (We would ask the team for this support. The parking pass was important because we wanted as few impediments as possible to ensure that the parents would be able to bring the excited recipient to the game.) I called the contacts that I had made on Leadership Oakland's "Education Day" and went to the assistant superintendent of schools to help iron out the student selection process. In order to receive a Stadium Scholarship, the student had to be nominated by their teacher based on effort or improvement and good citizenship.

I then proceeded to *stalk* Mr. Alioto and Mr. Attles. I was able to meet with David and his community relations team first. Within a few weeks of our initial meeting, the SSP, the Oakland A's, and Oakland Rotary

Club #3 presented the first Stadium Scholarships to 16 deserving kids and their families during a pre-game ceremony on the field. The A's not only provided tickets and passes, but they also gave $100.00 per child. The Rotary Club of Oakland also provided $100.00 per recipient at the first presentation.

Next, it was on to Al and the Golden State Warriors. He's a very nice guy. I believe I called him so many times that he agreed to see me just to stop me from calling. As a matter of fact, when we finally sat down to talk, I remember him saying nearly in frustration, "William. What is it?" As I explained the idea, Al stopped me in mid-sentence and called in his community relations manager. We set up the first in what would be a five-year fun run of Stadium Scholarship presentations.

To date, we have given away over 250 Stadium Scholarships to outstanding kids from the Oakland public school system. Just an idea, fueled by some nice people that might change some lives for the better.

The Over 90 survey. I came across the results of a survey conducted with people over the age of ninety. The survey posed the question, "If you could live your life over again, what would you do differently? What would *you* do? Would you work more? Make more money? Spend more time with your kids? Travel around the world?" The answer was simple and nearly unanimous. Most of the respondents stated that they would spend a larger portion of their time doing things that would make a positive difference in peoples' lives. They, in essence, said that they wanted people to remember them as helpful, concerned, giving, and compassionate people. They wanted to feel that the memory of their good deeds would live on when people thought of them after they were dead and gone. **What**

141

do you want people to say about you after you die? What do you want people to say about you now? What *do* they say about you now? You can begin your legacy today.

Hidden Benefit. There is another benefit to charitable activity. I call it the hidden benefit: good feelings. In fact, I have found that most people feel so good after giving of themselves that they will do it again. When I read books to the first-grade class at Malcolm X Elementary school (formerly Sir Francis Drake, where I completed the kindergarten and first grades) in Hunters Point for the annual African American Read-In Chain, I jokingly tell them that I had sat in that very same class, in fact in that very same chair over forty years ago. When I get them to see that I am like them, that I once lived where they live, and now I am just older, the light comes on for them. It is just cool. I see myself in them and they see themselves in me. After one of these sessions I am charged up. I'm full of good feelings for at least two weeks. *That's* the hidden benefit. It's the way *you* feel when you help others.

I promised myself when I got to this point of the book that I wouldn't beat the issue of active social awareness and charity to death. I challenge you to get out and help someone for two hours a month. We can change the world. I just believe that because of our history — the sacrifices that were made for all of us to be here today — it's our responsibility to do what we can to establish our own legacy of good deeds. If any of these ideas make sense to you, please share them with someone you care about.

THE FIVE CHARITABLE SECRETS

1. Contact a cause and make a monthly commitment of an hour or two. Tell them when you will be coming by to help.
2. Give yourself a trial period to decide if it is truly the particular charity you want to help.
3. Work hard and smart at becoming a valuable asset to the cause.
4. Make it as important for your schedule as any other item you do each month.
5. Have fun!

Attributes of Successful People

1) **Positive Thoughts — Successful People Have Positive Thought Patterns**. Feed your mind positive food, and it will grow positive actions. If your last waking thoughts at night are positive, chances are you will wake feeling excited and ready to seize the day. The great motivator and trainer Zig Ziglar once said, "Your attitude, not your aptitude, will determine your altitude."

2) **Written Goals---Most Successful People Write and/or Visualize Their Goals.** Write what you want, why you want it, how you are going to get it, when you will begin — and you are 90% there. Then read it daily. "Before you can score, you must have a goal."- Anonymous

3) **Immediate Focused Activity---Successful People Focus on and Actively Pursue Their Goals.** Once you have a clear goal, begin to achieve it *immediately.* Do something every single day towards your goal. Know that it is up to you to accomplish it. "I am only one, but I still am one. I cannot do everything, but I can still do something; and because I cannot do everything, I will not refuse to do the something that I can do."- Ms. Helen Keller

4) **Constant Mental Growth---Successful People are Always Learning.** Cut into your TV time. Learn something new every day-week-month-year. A book a month, a class per semester, a seminar or workshop per quarter — you must continue your "formal" academic learning. In addition, you must continue your "informal" life learning. Talk to, listen to, and learn from older people, younger people,

different people, successful people, homeless people, physically and mentally challenged people, academic people, life-learned people, healthy people, and sick people. A better way to do whatever you're trying to do exists; you just have to find it. Ideas and thoughts from others help you formulate your own. "I have learned silence from the talkative, tolerance from the intolerant, and kindness from the unkind."- Kahlil Gibran

5) **Consistent Persistence---Successful People Keep Going.** In perfecting the incandescent lamp, Thomas Edison and his research team experienced ten thousand failures before he finally succeeded. A friend of Edison's chanced to remark that ten thousand failures were a lot of failures; to which Edison replied, "I didn't fail ten thousand times. I successfully eliminated, ten thousand times, materials and combinations which wouldn't work."

6) **Honesty and Dependability---Successful People are Honest and Dependable.** In business as well as in personal life, news of dishonesty and unreliability travels literally at the speed of light. Can others count on you to do what you said you were going to do when you said you were going to do it? "A half-truth is a whole lie."- Jewish proverb. Ralph Waldo Emerson once said, "What you do speaks so loud that I cannot hear what you say."

7) **Energy---Successful People Keep Going.** All life requires energy, but a successful life requires megawatts of it. Develop habits that sustain and replenish your energy supply. "A dead fish can float downstream, but it takes a live one to swim upstream."- W.C. Fields

8) **Making a Difference---Successful People Take the Old and Turn it Into the New**. Create unique success. Study and learn from the past to create a new future. Don't copy failure. "The best way to predict the future is to create it."-Anonymous

9) **Humor.** Please, please, please try to have some fun everyday. Have a hearty, healthy belly laugh at least once but hopefully several times a day. "Laughter is inner jogging."-Anonymous

In the End....

Full Life Balance in all of its components has taught me essentially one thing: *I Am The One.* I am not surprised when I accomplish the unimaginable because *I Am the One.* I am not surprised when the blessings of the universe are showered on me: *I Am The One.* I am a child of the spirit: *I Am The One.* And *Full Life Balance* has taught me that for all the same reasons — *You Are The One.*

How can that be? Because the spirit, the force, the source is endless, boundless and limitless. There is enough for everyone to be the one. I am the only me. My thoughts, feelings, and actions have never been done exactly the way I do them. It is impossible for anyone to be exactly the one I am. *I Am The One.* And as you know, the same things apply to you. *You Are The One.* The way you harness the universe has never been done exactly this way, at exactly this time, in exactly this place. *You Are The One.*

You have choices. You can choose to think that you are small, ineffectual, and insignificant; and as a result, act accordingly. When you act this way, you expect to fail, you aim low, and you don't use all the power that is available to you. You are shocked when you are successful.

Conversely, when you acquire *Full Life Balance,* you expect success; you expect happiness; you expect a miracle. *Full Life Balance* helps you put yourself in position to be successful. It helps you get poised for the blessings of life.

You have some great things in front of you. Know it. Claim it. Just remember that your spirit, your body, your emotions, your mind, and your heart are all connected. So take care of them as if they were your

147

children. Please take care of *all* of them in order to Live Better Everyday®.

I pray that you now know that "It's all connected."

The Challenge

I asked earlier that if you found something in this book that made sense for you and your family to challenge yourself and do it for 90 days. To help you identify your challenge, please answer these few questions.

1. What is spirituality to you?

   _____

2. Do you think there is a being or spirit greater than you?

   _____

3. How do you demonstrate it?

   _____

4. If yes, how do you describe it?

   _____

5. If not, why not?

   _____

6. What does FLB mean to you?

   _____

7. Are you balanced?

   _____

8. If so, how did you achieve it?

   _____

9. If not, why not?

   _____

10. How will you stay balanced?

_____

11. What did you find helpful in this book?

_____

    a. _____

    b. _____

    c. _____

    d. _____

    e. _____

12. The Challenge: Based on what you have written, what 5 things are you going to do each day for the next 90 days?

    1. Spiritual

_____

    2. Physical

_____

    3. Emotional

_____

    4. Professional

_____

    5. Charitable

_____

13. What will you do today to begin?

_____

_____

NOTE: I would be honored if you would share your answers to these questions with me at **fulifebalance@yahoo.com**.

Epilogue

Well, here we are at the end. Thank you for giving me the most precious thing any of us has — your time. I gotta let you go now. This semester, I am teaching a Management Principles class. After I finish this last sentence, I am going to grade some student assignments; but I'm looking at my guitar and, once again, I'm feeling "funky." I will see you again. Be well and strive to "Live Better Everyday." ®

W

THE FIVE PHYSICAL SECRETS
Remember, it takes energy to live a successful life.
Remember the basics:

1. Diet, water, rest and exercise.
2. Physical, mental and cultural hobbies.
3. Self-preservation.
4. Prevention.
5. Enjoy yourself.

THE FIVE EMOTIONAL SECRETS
The emotional key may require the most work for most of us.

1. Assess our behavior.
2. Cleanse negative attitudes.
3. Model desirable behavior.
4. Forgive ourselves and others — honest, specific and timely.
5. Listen, thank, ask, tell, share and MAKE TIME.

THE FIVE PROFESSIONAL SECRETS

1. Know that it is not just what we do or how we do it or why we do it or how much we get paid to do it or how much we enjoy it — its all of these things, they are all connected.
2. Identify the thing that we are gifted to do.
3. Work harder and smarter to become better at our gift.
4. Apply the work harder and smarter adage to our entire life.
5. Develop mastery of our personal and professional habits.

THE FIVE SPIRITUAL SECRETS
This may be the most important stage of *Full Life Balance.*
1.   Develop a spiritual life perspective.
2.   Consciously seeking the positive source.
3.   Strive daily to do good, be good, and, through your thoughts and actions, show others (especially the children) the power of good.
4.   Avoid the mind and body traps that lie in your path.
5.   By using prayer, meditation and seeking the light, you can maintain and enhance your spiritual perspective.

THE FIVE CHARITABLE SECRETS

1.   Contact a cause and make a monthly commitment of an hour or two. Tell them when you will be coming by to help.
2.   Give yourself a trial period to decide if is truly the particular charity you want to help.
3.   Work hard and smart at becoming a valuable asset to the cause.
4.   Make it as important for your schedule as any other item you do each month.
5.   Have fun!

SUGGESTED READING

The Bible

The Koran

The Talmud

The Life Of The Buddah

The Greatest Salesman Who Ever Lived

Forty-Eight Laws of Power

Call of the Wild

The Invisible Man

Water For Elephants

Made in the USA
Charleston, SC
22 December 2014